BRIDGING TWO WORLDS

Supporting Newcomer and Refugee Youth

A GUIDE TO CURRICULUM IMPLEMENTATION AND INTEGRATION

Jan Stewart and Lorna Martin

Cover photography by David Lipnowski Photography and Naniece Ibrahim Photography
Design and layout by Lindsay Maclachlan, White Walnut Design

Bridging Two Worlds
Copyright © Stewart, J. and Martin, L. (2018)

Published by:
CERIC
Foundation House
Suite 300, 2 St. Clair Avenue East
Toronto, ON
M4T 2T5
Website: www.ceric.ca
Email: admin@ceric.ca

ISBN
Paperback: 978-1-988066-27-1
ePDF: 978-1-988066-28-8

Design and layout: Lindsay Maclachlan, White Walnut Design

The following photographs courtesy of www.pexels.com:
p. 140: Lorenzo Cafaro, Tim Gouw, Pixabay, freestocks.org
Cover photograph courtesy of Naniece Ibrahim (University of Winnipeg) and David Lipnowski

ACKNOWLEDGEMENTS

BRIDGING TWO WORLDS RESOURCE DEVELOPMENT AND CURRICULUM WRITERS

Dr. Jan Stewart, University of Winnipeg
Dr. Lorna Martin, University of Winnipeg

LESSON DEVELOPMENT LEADS AND ANALYTICS TEAM

Kari McCluskey, University of Winnipeg
Kirby Borgardt, University of Winnipeg
Dania El Chaar PhD (Candidate), University of Calgary

LESSON CONTRIBUTORS

Aliraza Alidina, University of Winnipeg
Brianna Hilman, Werklund School of Education, University of Calgary
Caroline Fisher, Winnipeg School Division
Chantelle Cotton, Winnipeg School Division
Jennifer Streilein, Seven Oaks School Division
Hua Que, Memorial University of Newfoundland

We also wish to acknowledge the contributions from the members of the three regional focus group consultations in Manitoba, Alberta, and Newfoundland.

PARTNERS

University of Winnipeg
University of Calgary
Memorial University of Newfoundland
Newcomers Employment and Education Development Services (N.E.E.D.S.) Inc., Manitoba
CERIC
Manitoba Education and Training
Refugee and Immigrant Council (RIAC)
International Centre for Innovation in Education (ICIE)

PROJECT FUNDERS

Social Sciences and Humanities Research Council of Canada
CERIC
Mitacs
University of Winnipeg
Werklund School of Education, University of Calgary

We would like to thank the many research assistants and contributors to this project, many of whom are not formally acknowledged herein, but who willingly shared their knowledge and expertise, and for whom the project team is grateful.

THE UNIVERSITY OF **WINNIPEG**

 **CERIC** Advancing Career Development in Canada | Promouvoir le développement de carrière au Canada

 UNIVERSITY OF CALGARY WERKLUND SCHOOL OF EDUCATION

 **MEMORIAL** UNIVERSITY

 Social Sciences and Humanities Research Council of Canada   Conseil de recherches en sciences humaines du Canada   **Canada**

TABLE OF CONTENTS

● ● ● ●

SECTION THREE: LEARNING OUTCOMES AND INSTRUCTIONAL IDEAS FOR ALL STUDENTS

INTRODUCTION

This book and the study upon which it is based grew out of the Canadian spirit of cultural diversity and inclusivity. The title, *Bridging Two Worlds: Supporting Newcomer and Refugee Youth*, reflects the guiding premise of professionals working with newcomer and refugee families in our country: to effectively support the growth and development of a healthy society and the independence of those within it, we must acknowledge and respect the diverse cultures and lived experiences of newcomers to Canada, beginning with children and youth. By building culturally responsive bridges to Canada in our school systems, we strengthen resiliency and address many of the challenges that face refugee and newcomer students.

In the first section of the text, we consider each of the themes that emerged from our research as they relate to school-based learning and teaching. While not all newcomers to Canada face the cumulative effects of trauma, interrupted learning, and new-language acquisition, all educators should be aware of how these affect human development and learning. The text discusses creating a welcoming classroom, trauma-informed care values, school-wide positive behaviour supports, the role of cultural brokers, and practices and policies that address the needs of refugee and newcomer students.

The second section focuses on educator competency—preparing and training teachers and counsellors to work with newcomer and refugee children and youth. We present relevant core competencies from the *Career Development Guidelines and Standards of Practice* and 30 sample lessons for educators. These lessons are correlated to both the Guidelines and Standards and to our research-based themes.

The book concludes with a section devoted to student learning outcomes for life/work development. Learning outcomes from the *Blueprint for Life/Work Designs* are provided with accompanying suggestions for instruction across all elementary and secondary grade levels, Kindergarten to Grade 12 (K-12).

The need for competent and culturally responsive career development programs and services begins in Canadian schools, with children and youth. Within the classroom setting, educators teach and use important constructs that smooth the transition from diverse countries of origin to diverse regions of Canada, beginning with universal design, multiple intelligences, and differentiated instruction. These support all students, not only those who struggle to learn or whose background includes refugee and newcomer experiences.

This book grew out of a three-year research program that investigated schools and communities in Calgary, Winnipeg, and St. John's to learn about the shared and disparate approaches to career development for refugee and newcomer children. This knowledge was intended to serve counsellors and teachers who provide career development programs and services and to help create stronger networks among community partners, universities, organizations, and schools throughout Canada. Interns who participated in this research program were a part of a multi-agency support network to facilitate the provision of career development programs and services for newcomer/refugee youth. Interns contributed to the development of recommended policies and best practices and the creation of activities and lesson plans for teachers and counsellors.

The overarching goal was to contribute new knowledge to the Canadian Education and Research Institute for Counselling (CERIC) and to equip teachers and counsellors with the knowledge and practical resources to provide career counselling to middle- and secondary-school newcomer and refugee youth in Canada.

Bridging Two Worlds offers data-informed curriculum development and instructional ideas that recognize and address educational gaps as well as cultural or experiential differences that impede progress. The research informing this resource was conducted between 2014 and 2017 and revealed nine thematic categories related to effective pedagogy and mental health supports:

1. Conflict Awareness
2. Social Determinants of Health
3. Peace and Sustainability
    a. Restorative Practices and Justice
    b. Equity
4. Refugee Characteristics
    a. Anger Management
    b. Stress
    c. Resiliency
    d. Who Is the Student?
5. Building Personal and Community Connections
6. Cultural Competency/Culturally Safe and Responsive Teaching
    a. Listening, Empathy, and Perspective-Taking
    b. Counselling Skills
    c. Expressive Arts
    d. Storytelling
7. Trauma-Sensitivity, Mental Health Awareness, and Crisis Response
    a. Mental Health
    b. Loss and Grief
8. Career Planning and Career Development
9. Teacher Self-Care

These themes are described in detail on pages 16-21.

* * * * *

PURPOSE AND GOALS

Various programs and services have been introduced in Canada to address the career needs of newcomer adults; however, there is a lack of research that examines career decision-making for newcomer and refugee youth at the middle- and secondary-school level. This research was designed to look specifically at what educators and school counsellors could do to foster and facilitate informed career decision-making for newcomer and refugee youth. Because some schools do not have a designated counsellor, we intended to develop resources and training materials that could be used by resource and classroom teachers who also provide career-related services to youth. Research conducted with immigrant clients suggested that many intra-individual, relational, and contextual obstacles hindered adaptation to a new country (Elez, 2014). Research in Canada that focused on the educational needs of refugee children noted a void in adequate career-development programs and services for refugee children and youth (MacNevin, 2012; Stewart, 2017a, 2014, 2011).

We collected data from three cities across Canada—Calgary, Alberta; Winnipeg, Manitoba; and St. John's, Newfoundland—through observation, semi-structured interviews, and focus groups. The project design included a reciprocal process of investigating, learning, and problem solving with participants, investigators, collaborators, and partners—we hoped it would be mutually beneficial to community stakeholders and career-development counsellors and have an impact on both sectors. The partnering of scholars, practitioners, government representatives, and community organizations provided the foundation for a long-term research program with the potential to expand in scope to include additional provinces and cities. Through community forums and consultative workshops, participants in this research program developed recommendations for policy and practice—locally, provincially, and nationally. Together, this interdisciplinary exchange of knowledge enhanced our understanding of the complex career-development issues affecting newcomer/refugee students and allowed for the development of best practices and principles with the potential to improve the capacity of career practitioners and career counsellors. The regional focus group consultations and the national/international dissemination provided venues for the exchange of information, creation of new knowledge, and sharing of findings. The overarching goal of this research was to provide school counsellors with the knowledge and resources to provide more informed and culturally responsive career development and guidance to newcomer/refugee youth.

● ● ● ● ●

RESEARCH PHASES AND OUTCOMES

PHASE 1

May 2015–August 2015

The purpose of this initial phase was to gather information on how various communities support the career development of newcomer and refugee youth and to explore gaps in the provision of services and programs. The researchers and the interns in each city began by conducting 30–45 semi-structured interviews with individuals from the five ecological systems that interact with and influence students (see Ecological Systems). The co-investigators—Dr. Jan Stewart (principal), Dr. Tom Ricento, and Dr. Xuemei Li—coordinated data collection for their individual sites in each city, and the principal investigator coordinated the analysis of the data collected from all cities. A total of 108 interviews were conducted in this phase across the three provinces. The collaborators and partners in each city had an active role in gaining access to the participants, particularly those in the mesosystem, exosystem, and macrosystem, and they worked collaboratively with their co-investigator to collect, analyze, and interpret the data. The co-investigators and interns met every four weeks.

PHASE 2

September 2015–February 2016

To gather data specific on how schools support the career development of refugee students, more individual interviews were conducted: 50 in Calgary, 50 in St. John's, and 118 in Winnipeg. The 218 participants interviewed in this phase consisted of

---

● ● ● ●

ECOLOGICAL SYSTEMS

Humans develop in relation to various contexts or systems. In our investigation of the factors that influence refugee and newcomer students, we used Urie Brontenbrenner's bioecological model of those systems (Bronfenbrenner, 2001). As summarized and adapted by Stewart (2011), the model consists of five systems:

- The **nanosystem** is "a close, interpersonal relationship or network that is integral to connecting the individual to the microsystem" (Stewart, 2011, p. 135). Examples of a nanosystem include a parent, a coach, and a best friend.
- The **microsystem** is the immediate environment in which a person lives and includes his or her closest relationships. Families, sports teams, and peer groups are examples of microsystems.
- The **mesosystem** refers to linkages or connections among the various microsystems in a person's life, such as the linkages between a person's family and peer group, or a student's school experiences and family.
- The **exosystem** represents events that occur in more distant systems that indirectly affect a person's experiences. Examples of exosystems includes friends of the family, community members, social agencies, and neighbours.
- The **macrosystem** represents the ideologies or attitudes of the culture in which the other systems exist. This includes the values, customs, and laws of the society.

teachers, newcomer/refugee students, Canadian-born students, school administrators, and school-division consultants. In addition, focus groups were conducted in each city: refugee students, school counsellors, parents, teachers, and school leaders. Focus-group interviews investigated core competencies that needed to be developed to better prepare counsellors who work with newcomer/refugee youth. Interns helped conduct the interviews and co-facilitate the focus groups.

PHASE 3
March 2016–July 2016
Collaborators and investigators collected additional information about support systems and resources to meet the specific needs of refugee students. The data from Phases 1 and 2 were analyzed and preliminary findings were articulated. Participants from Phases 1 and 2 with knowledge and interest in program/lesson development (e.g., employment service facilitators, refugee support workers) were identified as stakeholders. The interns and the investigators worked with these stakeholders to create resources (manuals, lessons, strategies) to meet the identified training/development needs of pre-service and in-service career counsellors. These resources were drafted and discussed at regional focus-group consultations. Approximately 20–30 suggested learning activities were co-developed for use with pre-service or in-service teachers and counsellors in university settings or school divisions.

PHASE 4
July 2016–November 2016
All study participants were invited to attend a regional focus group in each city. Approximately 85 participants in total took part—20 each in St. John's and Calgary, and 45 in Winnipeg (more participants were added in Winnipeg due to interest from the various stakeholder groups). Participants included career counsellors, research partners, collaborators, investigators, students, and stakeholders. Participants reviewed and contributed to the development of the resources drafted in Phase 3 and generated action plans for their communities. Action plans included suggestions for policies, programs, and services to support career development for newcomer/refugee youth. The regional focus groups were recorded and later transcribed, coded, and analyzed. Lessons and resources were revised according to feedback from the regional focus groups.

PHASE 5
December 2016–February 2017
A three-day national focus group consultation was originally planned for Winnipeg. However, the Manitoba Government requested a series of four roundtable discussions with approximately 250 various stakeholders. Due to the overlap between events—many of the same stakeholders would have been invited to both—and the difficulty in getting participants to commit to a three-day event, the national focus group was cancelled and the team used the funding to travel to Ottawa and New York to promote the work nationally and internationally. In this way, the team disseminated the work to key associations and organizations and to a wider audience.

PHASE 6
March 2017–July 2017
Results from this research program and the regional focus groups were further disseminated to academic scholars, industry, practitioners, and policy-makers. Researchers and interns shared findings at provincial and national conferences (Cannexus, Canadian Society for the Study of Education, Canadian Counselling and Psychotherapy Association); through professional development seminars (webinars, workshops) for practitioners; and through journal articles, media interviews, and newsletter articles. In addition, a pilot

Career/Life Planning course was taught as a combined graduate/undergraduate course at the University of Winnipeg and will be offered again in 2018/19.

The University of Winnipeg held a summer institute and major conference attracting over 275 participants from July 12-15, 2017. Courses and breakout sessions relating to the thematic areas identified in the research (see pp. 16-21) were taught or presented. Five keynote sessions throughout the conference also linked to the thematic areas.

Table 1. Research phases and outcomes

Phase	Outcomes
1	• 108 interviews completed and transcribed (30–45 per city) • 10 observations of community or school career-support programs • 1 day-long focus group with career development practitioners from across Canada • initial data analysis results documented with NVivo software
2	• 218 individual interviews with newcomer/refugee students and school/division staff completed and transcribed • 5 focus groups in each city • data analysis results (codes and models) completed using NVivo software
3	• analysis of data from Phases 1 and 2 • stakeholders identified from among the participants in Phases 1 and 2 • resources for career counsellors and teachers drafted and discussed
4	• 3 focus groups (1 per city); approximately 85 participants in total • drafts of resources for career counsellors and teachers peer-reviewed and revised • data collected, transcribed, and analyzed; ongoing team-based analysis of data • content for curriculum developed
5	• team presentation of findings at the American Educational Research Association (AERA) conference in Washington, DC; dissemination of findings at other national and international conferences • curriculum document drafted • data from all 3 cities merged and coding reports generated
6	• dissemination of findings • Career/Life Planning course piloted at the University of Winnipeg; will be offered again in 2018/19

This guide, available online and in print, is the final outcome of the three-year research program. It provides an overview of the research program, recommendations for policy and practice, and career development lessons specifically written for counsellors and teachers who work with newcomer/refugee youth.

Dissemination of the findings from this study is expected to continue through 2018 at various conferences, symposia, and seminars.

SECTION ONE

UNDERSTANDING THE NEEDS

• • • • •

RESEARCH FINDINGS: KEY THEMES

Nine key themes and 12 sub-themes emerged when we categorized the data collected during our study. Themes include the social determinants of health, social justice and equity, trauma-informed practices, counselling skills, and educator self-care.

1. **CONFLICT AWARENESS.** Participants in the study were consistent in their determination that "teachers need to know where (students) are coming from, what is the history of conflict in their home country, and how students have been affected by war." This awareness is critical to building the relationships and alliances that encourage learning and growth. While increased awareness of war-affected areas of the world is important, it is even more pertinent to recognize the signs and symptoms of mental health and learning concerns in individual children.

   Not all children and youth who have emigrated from a war-affected country and have refugee or newcomer status will have been affected to the same degree or in the same way as siblings, other family members, or unrelated students from the same country. The respondents in the study confirmed that, to be highly effective, schools need to be trauma sensitive and as supportive of refugee and newcomer students as they would be of any student with an unknown or commonplace background. Teachers must be alert to potential unconscious biases that may lead them to generalize the experiences of students from abroad without direct evidence, or to link common behavioural and learning difficulties to a refugee or newcomer student without functional assessments and an evidence-based decision-making process. Many refugee and newcomer students are resilient and stable in their learning and transition to a new land and culture.

2. **SOCIAL DETERMINANTS OF HEALTH.** The health of Canadians' is directly affected by factors that include how income and wealth are distributed; employment status; the conditions of work where it is available; health and social services; and the quality and availability of education, food, and housing. In most cases, these social determinants of health, or living conditions, are beyond the control of refugee and newcomer families in Canada; they are most frequently determined by the communities in which individuals live, work, and go to school. Respondents in the study indicated that increased understanding of the inequities in access to community services and supports, adequate housing, food, and employment—and of potential solutions to these inequities—helps schools and school systems to support teachers as they work with refugee and newcomer students. Making referral agents and resources easily available to teachers enables them to help their students overcome obstacles to learning, aids in transitions, and supports positive experiences in their communities in particular, and in Canada in general.

3. **PEACE AND SUSTAINABILITY.** The study findings confirmed the importance of peace and sustainability in classrooms and school systems. Respondents indicated that teachers need to know how to infuse concepts from peace education and education for sustainable development into their practice. These concepts include restorative practices and equity training.

   a. **Restorative Practices and Justice.** Teachers need to know the language and principles of restorative practices and restorative justice and how to introduce these concepts into their classrooms. Conflicts and misbehaviours should be viewed as opportunities for social and emotional learning. Teachers need to know how to help students repair and restore relationships.

   b. **Equity.** Teachers in the study indicated a need for professional development (PD) focused on equity. As one respondent said, "we had PD in the early days around equity.... And one of the things for best practice in teaching is to differentiate and to integrate and do inquiry." Keeping the needs of students and their cultures at the forefront is key to successful teaching and learning. As one teacher described, "You're really trying to make sure [the students] get opportunities within the classroom, because we can't control what happens out there. We can control what happens here.... What we are doing, is trying to build equity."

4. **REFUGEE CHARACTERISTICS.** The most prevalent characteristics of refugees become apparent when one understands the underlying conditions common to so many of them. Students with refugee backgrounds tend to have had limited schooling, protracted and negative experiences during the exodus journey, and interrupted social and academic development. These factors create challenges to be overcome in all areas: educational, psychosocial, environmental, and academic. One study participant, a teacher, distilled the considerations that are required to support incoming students: "This is what a refugee centre is like ... this child might be old enough to be in a Grade 5 or 6 classroom, but [has] never been in school before, or only experienced school in a refugee camp. So, what does that kind of school experience look like? How can we then support them to be in this kind of school experience?"

Students who have had complicated migration experiences often exhibit emotional/behavioural attributes that schools must be attentive to, and resolve.

   a. **Anger.** The study findings confirmed that teachers need to know how to respond to children who are misbehaving or acting out in class. Skills in effectively de-escalating conflict, both internal and external, are key to supporting students who display symptoms consistent with frustration, anger, and sadness or depression.

   b. **Stress.** Many refugee students are experiencing stress due to multiple layers of challenges. Respondents indicated that teachers need a greater understanding of how to promote stress reduction and relaxation techniques, and how to make these a part of the daily routine in schools. Relevant learning outcomes in health curricula are often helpful; focused instruction and supports are available through comprehensive and developmental guidance and counselling programs, and referrals to school counsellors, school psychologists, and social workers.

   c. **Resiliency.** Recognizing the balance between risk and resiliency in a student's experience and accepting each student's understanding of his or her situation is the starting point for determining areas of strength in that student. What is resiliency? How do we foster resiliency? How can teachers focus on strengths and not deficits? What is it that allows some individuals to be highly resilient and possess incredible coping skills, while others with the same or a similar experience become highly susceptible to mental health problems and are deemed at "high risk" for additional problems in their lifetimes? According to respondents in the study, these questions should guide teachers to locating and employing effective supports for students, based on their individual contexts and unique personalities, life conditions, and academic functioning.

   d. **Who is the E/FAL Student?** Teachers often recognize students who have English or French as an additional language by their literacy levels in the dominant language of the classroom. While many refugee and newcomer students may have limited facility in the language of the classroom, they may also have limited facility in their first language (for reasons that include a paucity of educational opportunity, migration conditions that inhibited reading and writing, and limited access to formal education due to gender-based or economic-based constraints). As one study participant indicated, low literacy levels and facility in English or

French are not unique to refugee and newcomer students; students with other backgrounds and in other communities experience these also: "[There] are all these things that I didn't realize fall under EAL. Whether [students] were on a reserve and how many years behind [provincial curriculum outcomes for literacy] and depending on how much they talk at home in their native tongue, all of these things we need to know." Improving literacy should be a goal for all students.

5. **BUILDING PERSONAL AND COMMUNITY CONNECTIONS.** Increasing personal resilience is often associated with strengthening the network of support available to refugee and newcomer students. Respondents in the study confirmed this: that when schools build connections with the refugee community, personal connections with and for students increase, their sense of belongingness is enhanced, and opportunities for creating success multiply.

6. **CULTURAL COMPETENCY: CULTURALLY SAFE AND RESPONSIVE TEACHING.** Schools and school divisions create policies to produce culturally safe and responsive environments for teaching. These policies and their procedures within classrooms diminish incidents of violence, exclusion, bullying, and absenteeism. When schools provide safe and caring environments that are sensitive to the needs of culturally, linguistically, and religiously diverse learners, the result is a more inclusive school and classroom. Accommodating the needs of students from diverse backgrounds can seem daunting. Simple solutions to what appear to be complex problems are available in a series of implementation documents from provincial ministries of education. See table 2 for some examples.

Table 2. Creating inclusive schools and classrooms: A sample of provincial implementation documents

British Columbia	*Making space: Teaching for diversity and social justice throughout the K–12 curriculum.* British Columbia Education and Training, 2008. https://www.bced.gov.bc.ca/irp/pdfs/making_space/mkg_spc_intr.pdf
Manitoba	*Responding to religious diversity in Manitoba's schools: A guide for educators* (2015). Manitoba Education and Advanced Learning, 2015. http://www.edu.gov.mb.ca/k12/docs/support/religious_diversity/full_doc.pdf *Safe and caring schools: Respect for human diversity policies.* Manitoba Education and Advanced Learning, 2015. http://www.edu.gov.mb.ca/k12/docs/support/human_diversity/document.pdf
Ontario	Equity and inclusive education in Ontario schools: Guidelines for policy development and implementation. Ontario Ministry of Education, 2014. http://www.edu.gov.on.ca/eng/policyfunding/inclusiveguide.pdf

a. **Listening, Empathy, and Perspective-Taking.** Teachers are well-versed in teaching with diversity in mind. Multiple intelligences, universal design, and differentiated instruction are well-known concepts in the teaching community. For teachers of refugee and newcomer students, it is equally important to listen to student stories; to empathize with their plight, their hopes, their fears; and to consider goal-setting, life adjustment, and the meaning of success from a variety of perspectives. As one study participant indicated, "I think the biggest lesson I've had to learn is to see people as people. And if we want to help, especially people who are new to this country, we can't just start with the content. We have to start with the person." Listening, reflecting, summarizing, prompting, and guiding are key skills in making a positive difference in the lives and the learning for students who are new to the Canadian system of education, the Canadian environment, and Canadian culture.

b. **Counselling Skills.** Teachers are not generally qualified counsellors and cannot be expected to serve as such. It is helpful to all students, however, if their teachers understand and use active listening in the classroom. Additionally, according to study findings, teachers must recognize behavioural indicators of mental health difficulties or adjustment issues that may require the support of qualified mental health and/or educational psychology professionals. School counsellors, school psychologists, and social workers, as well as settlement workers, are professionals to whom teachers or schools may commonly refer students. In the study, one teacher said, "I don't remember if we really had any training in counselling at all to deal with issues like this, especially for the inner city, where there are a lot of people like refugees and immigrants. I think there should be a component in pre-service teacher programs, where pre-service teachers are trained to provide basic counselling skills."

c. **Expressive Arts.** The use of creative expression and expressive arts were noted by respondents in the study as being of great use to children who have experienced involuntary displacement, violence, or trauma. Many expressive arts activities can be easily woven into curricular outcomes in all areas. They include clay-work, painting, collage-building, dancing, drawing, poetry and various other forms of creative expression.

d. **Storytelling.** Participants frequently cited the need to foster storytelling by refugees to Canadians, but also between refugee communities and by Canadians to refugees. They referred to this as a reciprocal process of learning and understanding together. They also discussed the danger of a single story—the harm of only focusing on the trauma story and the need to articulate the survival story. The freedom and safety to tell one's story and to be heard without judgment has proven to be beneficial in enhancing self-concept, finding equilibrium, and adapting to the immersive environment of Canadian schools.

7. **TRAUMA-SENSITIVITY, MENTAL HEALTH AWARENESS, AND CRISIS RESPONSE.** Study participants acknowledged the prevalence of potentially traumatic experiences in students' countries of origin, in their transition to Canada, and in their new Canadian communities. Participants noted the importance of creating and using flexible frameworks to support both the academic and social components of school life. For example, universal supports that are mindful of the needs of all students, including refugee and newcomer students, were important to respondents in supporting students with trauma, mental health, and crisis response. Many refugee and newcomer students have had traumatic experiences, and participants articulated the need for teachers to be better prepared to create safe and trauma-sensitive classrooms. Said one teacher, "I know there's lots of trauma, the way I cope with trauma, it may be different from the way kids cope, right? Well, I know that. I believe the triggers are very essential for us to know, [be]cause for many, you know, loud noise [is startling and difficult]. Like, anything that is explosive, would trigger [a trauma response]." Another study participant focused on the importance of professional learning—not just knowing what the individual student's difficulty

may be, but what it means for that particular student and for an effective learning environment. The teacher said, "They are suffering PTSD, and what does that mean? What does it look like? ... I think we need PD on that."

Based on the work of Cole et al. (2005), educators now understand that trauma is not an event. Rather, it is a response to a stressful experience in which a person's ability to cope is dramatically undermined. Biologically, the stress response is life affirming. From time to time, the stress response occurs when there is no clear and present danger. It is in these cases that we consider assessing students for post-traumatic stress, anxiety conditions or disorders, and depression. In collaboration and consultation with a mental health professional, teachers can help students to learn, apply, consolidate, and adapt coping skills to address the re-lived trauma that impedes learning.

The role of the teacher is supportive. The teacher's focus is on the student's educational success and his/her integration into the social fabric of the learning environment. Effective teachers in this role are attentive to emotional and physical safety, inclusion, empowerment, trust, personal choice, and collaboration. It is the role of the clinical mental-health specialist to intervene therapeutically with the student to address trauma reactions and to reduce symptoms that negatively affect mental health and wellness, learning, remembering, and socializing.

    a.   **Mental Health.** One in five Canadians will experience a mental health issue in their lifetime (Health Canada, 2002). Furthermore, in 2012, 17% of the population aged 15 and older reported having a mental health care need that required counselling, information, medication, or other intervention (Sunderland & Findlay, 2013). Statistically, it is reasonable to expect that the population of refugee and newcomer families will have at least the same, if not higher, incidence rates due to the effects of displacement, instability, trauma, and reduced access to the social determinants of health. Early recognition and timely treatment result in optimal relief. School systems and the professionals who work within them are well-situated to respond to the mental health needs of refugee and newcomer children and youth when they have sufficient education and training on the subject.

Schools typically have policies and procedures related to crisis prevention, intervention, and postvention. Schools in which there is awareness and understanding of mental health issues—their typical presentation and the recommended responses that facilitate a return to mental stability and readiness for learning—can act to increase the inclusion and sense of belongingness for all students in their lesson planning, teaching, learning, and assessment. Many crises can be averted when the social, educational, and athletic fabric of schools includes all students, regardless of their country of origin, education, or mental health status. It is vital to recognize that mental health issues can affect all learners, and to recognize and address behavioural, social, and academic changes in performance with sensitivity and immediacy.

    b.   **Loss and Grief.** Refugee students may have lost family members due to death, or be separated from family members by forced migrations. The whereabouts and condition of family members may be completely unknown. Respondents in the study indicated that teachers need to understand loss and know how to support students who are grieving the death of, or separation from, a loved one.

8. **CAREER PLANNING AND CAREER DEVELOPMENT.** Career Planning is life planning. Teachers in the study indicated a need for information about apprenticeships, internships, mentoring, and the world of work. They also articulated a need to know how to uncover the values, interests, skills, and attitudes of students. Teachers need background in these areas to better foster career development with students. Fortunately, the competency areas related to career planning and career development—

the activity of forward-looking and future-seeking—are well-researched and available to teachers in curricular form. *The Canadian Standards and Guidelines for Career Development Practitioners* (Canadian Council for Career Development, 2012) set out the core competencies for those working in the field. For students, the *Blueprint for Life/Work Designs* (2010) offers age- and stage-appropriate outcomes which are commonly included in curricula across Canada, from kindergarten through grade 12 . As one respondent from an NGO said, "Career development is just another thing to be taught in school. My view was schools—which I separate from education—have a role to play."

9. **TEACHER SELF-CARE.** The importance of teacher self-care reverberated across the data in the study. Participants articulated the critical role of educators in the integration and success of refugee and newcomer students and the attendant requirement for them to be able to function as advocates and trusted allies in addition to teachers and mentors. These roles require teachers to ensure the robustness of their own mental health status. To be able to support students, teachers must be resilient, forward-thinking, and able to address their own stress levels. Avoiding or mitigating vicarious trauma and compassion fatigue was seen as a key factor in the ability of teachers to better support students.

LINKAGES AND PROCESSES THAT AFFECT SUCCESS

The challenges that face refugee and newcomer students are multiple, varied, and often unique to their background and current living and working conditions. To increase opportunities for success in addressing and overcoming barriers, schools and systems in Canada receiving these students must

- recognize and address educational gaps and cultural or experiential differences that impede progress.

- have sufficient staff—or access to staff and/or referral agents—to assist in identifying indicators of common mental health difficulties and common educational difficulties. These staff or referral agents may include teacher leaders, school counsellors, consultants, settlement workers, and school psychologists among others.

- adequately support all students. Within the classroom setting, teachers must recognize the importance of, and implement, constructs related to universal design, multiple intelligences, and differentiated instruction. This process supports all students in the classroom and school environment, not only those students who struggle to learn or who have a background that includes refugee and newcomer experiences.

Jan Stewart (2011) provides a visual representation of the linkages and processes that commonly affect the success of refugee and newcomer students (see figure 1).

Figure 1. Adjustment challenges for refugee and newcomer students.

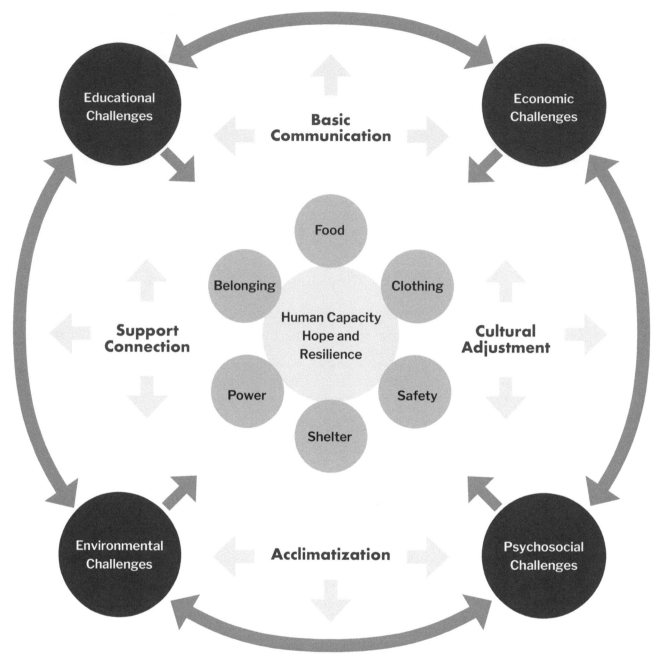

(Jan Stewart, 2011)

While the challenges shown in figure 1 affect a refugee or newcomer student's ability to succeed in school, it must be remembered that these students have already demonstrated keen skills in survival, adaptation, and resiliency. The protective factors that served them well in finding their way to Canada are the same factors that school staff must consider when supporting students in their new setting. Positive and still-useful coping skills and strategies must be encouraged; coping skills that enabled survival in prior times and settings but that would be culturally or practically inappropriate in the new setting must pro-gressively give way to more developmentally and socially acceptable means of addressing educational, economic, environmental, and psychosocial challenges. It is important to remember that maladaptive behaviours or responses to challenges may have previously been life-saving in the experience of the refugee or newcomer student. Teachers and other school staff must be patient and understanding in setting realistic goals for positive change. Simply demanding that a refugee or newcomer student "stop" a behaviour is inadequate and counterproductive. It is more constructive and helpful to instruct the student in adaptive behaviours to "replace" behaviours that do not suit the new situation in Canada.

Compounding the adjustment challenges and stressors upon arrival in Canada are factors that pre-date arrival, all of which combine to affect mental health. Kirmayer et al. (2011) groups migration-related factors that influence mental health into three categories: pre-migration, the migration process, and post-migration experiences (see table 3.)

Table 3. Factors related to migration that affect the mental health of refugee and newcomer students

Factors related to migration that affect mental health		
Pre-migration	**Migration**	**Post-Migration**
Adult		
Economic, educational, and occupational status in country of origin	Trajectory (route, duration)	Uncertainty about immigration or refugee status
Disruption of social support, roles, and network	Exposure to harsh living conditions (e.g., refugee camps)	Unemployment or underemployment
Trauma (type, severity, perceived level of threat, number of episodes)	Exposure to violence	Loss of social status
Political involvement (commitment to a cause)	Disruption of family and community networks	Loss of family and community social supports
	Uncertainty about outcome of migration	Concern about family members left behind and possibility for reunification
		Difficulties in language learning, acculturation, and adaptation (e.g., change in sex roles)
Child		
Age and developmental stage at migration	Separation from caregiver	Stresses related to family's adaptation
Disruption of education	Exposure to violence	Difficulties with education in new language
Separation from extended family and peer networks	Exposure to harsh living conditions (e.g., refugee camps)	Acculturation (e.g., ethnic and religious identity; sex role conflicts; intergenerational conflict within family)
	Poor nutrition	Discrimination and social exclusion (at school or with peers)
	Uncertainty about future	

(Kirmayer et al., 2011, p. E961)

THE EFFECTS OF TRAUMA AND INTERRUPTED LEARNING

CHILDREN AND TRAUMA

Trauma is a response to a stressful experience in which the person's capacity to cope is undermined (Cole et al., 2005). "A traumatic event is one that threatens injury, death, or the physical integrity of self or others and also causes horror, terror, or helplessness at the time it occurs" (American Psychological Association [APA], 2008). Traumatic events can be acute, happening only once, such as a serious accident, disaster, or the sudden or violent death of a loved one. Traumatic events can also happen repeatedly over a period of time. Examples of such events might include war, abductions, detainment, family violence, emotional abuse, physical abuse, or sexual abuse. Both acute trauma and trauma that occurs over time are made worse for children when their caretakers fail to provide support and care (Diehl, 2013). Children have tremendous capacity to be resilient, particularly after a one-time event. Over time, and when support and help are provided, stress dissipates and the child is able to heal and recover.

It is common for children who have refugee backgrounds to be exposed to more than one trauma and to have this happen over an extended period of time. Some children have been separated from their family while others may not have a trusted caregiver who can provide continuing support. In these instances, children are more vulnerable to post-traumatic stress disorder, anxiety, and other related psychological problems.

The APA (2008) estimates that a significant number of children in the United States are exposed to traumatic life events such as abuse, violence, terrorism, disaster, or traumatic loss. It is estimated that 1 in every 4 children attending US schools has been exposed to a traumatic event that can affect their learning and behaviour (National Child Traumatic Stress Network, 2008, p. 4). The 2008 Canadian Incidence Study of Reported Child Abuse and Neglect conducted by the Public Health Agency of Canada (2010) reported 1.4% of Canadian children experienced significant maltreatment including exposure to violence and neglect, physical abuse, emotional maltreatment, and sexual abuse. Research indicates that the majority of children who have been exposed to trauma are never identified and subsequently do not receive treatment or assistance (APA, 2008); the consequences for children include a significant increase in risk of post-traumatic stress disorder, depression, substance-use disorders, and mental health issues (Kilpatrick et al., 2003).

REFUGEES AND TRAUMA

The United Nations High Commissioner for Refugees (UNHCR, 2017) reports that there are now 65.6 million people worldwide forcibly displaced from their homes—nearly twice the population of Canada (Statistics Canada, 2016). Out of this number, 22.5 million are refugees and over half are children under the age of 18 (UNHCR, 2017). Some youth have been born and lived their entire lives in refugee camps. Very few of the displaced people find a permanent home and some who leave the insecurity, in search of safety, face perilous consequences.

The refugee experience is rife with harrowing stories of loss, fear, insecurity, trauma, abuse, exploitation, torture, separation from family, and deprivation of basic needs. Displaced and conflict-affected persons suffer physical and mental-health consequences of their plight in both the short term and the long term (Mollica, Brooks, Ekbald, & McDonald, 2015). Arrival in a host country can represent a new beginning and hope for a better future, but challenges persist and memories are not forgotten (Stewart, 2011). Newly arrived refugees experience stresses related to economic difficulties, academic struggles, fear of deportation, substandard housing, and the overall challenge of adjusting to a new country. Collectively, these stressors contribute to the overall risk for developing mental health difficulties (Ehntholt & Yule, 2006).

While there is conflicting discourse related to the degree to which refugees may or may not have experienced trauma, it is generally agreed that refugees have endured particular experiences that have pushed them involuntarily out of their country or across borders because of conflict or persecution (Russell, 2002). Because of the worldwide increase in displaced persons and the commitment of the Government of Canada to support more refugees, the demographics of Canadian schools and communities are changing. Educators need to be properly trained to support children and youth who have been exposed to trauma—in some cases prolonged and pervasive trauma. This does not mean that educators need to be therapists or counsellors. Rather, all school staff need to know how to approach children who are suffering or hurting, and they need to know how to listen, comfort, and respond, without causing harm.

Participants interviewed as part of this study indicated that they believe refugees suffer from a "triple trauma effect." Many refugees have experienced a traumatic event(s) in their home country such as armed conflict, abductions, terrorism, detainment, violence, or persecution. They experience trauma a second time in the transition to life in a refugee camp, or in a period of uncertainty, when living in temporary (second-country) settlement situations. Newly arrived refugees might experience trauma a third time while settling into a new country. Study participants with refugee backgrounds discussed feeling marginalized, experiencing racism and discrimination, and feeling a loss of career and social status.

Reports of the prevalence of post-traumatic stress disorder (PTSD) among refugees varies wildly—from as low as 5% to as high as 89% (Fazel, Wheeler, & Danesh, 2005). A meta-analysis of studies related to mental health of refugees reports the prevalence of PTSD is 30.6% and the prevalence of depression is 30.8% (Mollica, 2011). It is estimated that approximately 40% of young refugees may have psychiatric disorders, including PTSD, depression, and anxiety-related issues (Hodes, 2000).

A report from the Canadian Paediatric Society (2016) puts the prevalence of PTSD among refugee children at approximately 11%. Numerous factors can affect the prevalence of PTSD, such as the severity and duration of the trauma. Based on the work of Cole et al. (2005) the characteristics of the individual, the environment, and the nature of the traumatic event all influence how the child responds to trauma. There are also psychosocial issues that influence resilience and the child's ability to cope (Cole et al., 2005).

Characteristics of individual children that influence their resilience include their

- age and stage of development.
- personality and coping mechanisms.
- intellectual capacity.

Characteristics of the environment that influence a child's resilience include

- the immediate support provided by the caregivers or those close to the child.
- the attitudes of caregivers.
- the degree of safety provided to the child immediately following the trauma.
- the overarching attitudes and political views.
- the values of the community.

Children are at a higher risk for lasting effects of trauma when they experience low social support and poor family functioning after the event (Diehl, 2013).

• • • •

RECOGNIZING AND RESPONDING TO DISTRESS IN CHILDREN AND YOUTH

The Manitoba Government has developed three fact sheets to increase awareness of the signs of distress in children, youth, and adults among service providers. These are available at http://www.manitoba.ca/health/primarycare/providers/srh.html#mh. One of these, Optimizing Well-being and Responding to Emotional Distress of Children and Youth, is reprinted by permission in this guide (see Appendix, pp. 219-222).

The nature of the traumatic event also influences the trauma response. Characteristics include

- the frequency, intensity, severity, and duration of the event(s).
- the degree of humiliation and violation.
- the level of terror and violence.
- the persistence of threat and the proximity to the event (in the case of the child not being a targeted victim).

Resilience is not permanent, nor does it necessarily transfer from one environment to another. Even seemingly "resilient" children need support and understanding.

RECOGNIZING PTSD IN CHILDREN AND YOUTH

Post-traumatic stress disorder (PTSD) is a psychiatric descriptor for persons who exhibit a cluster of trauma responses to an event. Described in the *Diagnostic Statistical Manual-5* (DSM-5) of the American Psychiatric Association (2013) under the heading of Trauma- and Stressor-Related Disorders, the diagnostic criteria for PTSD includes four system clusters: intrusion, avoidance, negative alterations in cognitions and mood, and alterations in arousal and reactivity. These clusters of trauma responses are considered through the lens of duration, function, and whether any other condition or substance could have created the symptoms observed.

The DSM-5 is the first edition of the DSM to include a preschool subtype for PTSD. This subtype considers the behavioural responses of children aged 6 years and younger. Dr. M. Scheeringa (2013) notes that young children are exposed to many types of traumatic experiences that place them at risk for PTSD:

- abuse
- witnessing interpersonal violence
- motor vehicle accidents
- experiences of natural disasters
- conditions of war
- dog bites
- invasive medical procedures

For refugee and newcomer students (as well as students who have lived in the same community in Canada for many years), several of these experiences may be at play simultaneously. According to Scheeringa (2013), because "young children have emerging abstract cognitive and verbal expression capacities, research has shown that the criteria need to be more behaviorally anchored and developmentally sensitive to detect PTSD" in very young children. Educators and mental-health providers must be sensitized to the change in typical reactions of children and youth at the time of the trauma-inducing events. Rather than searching for symptoms of intrusive thoughts in very young children, it is more appropriate to look for reactions that shows distress. (Depending on the individual, these may include over-excitement, sudden withdrawal, avoidance, loss of interest, and detachment.) Older children may demonstrate a "sense of a foreshortened future" and an "inability to recall an important aspect of the event," but younger children are more likely to exhibit extreme temper tantrums or sudden developmental challenges in previously attained age- and stage-related milestones.

THE TRAUMA-INFORMED SCHOOL

The school is often the first, the most influential, and sometimes the only system the refugee child is in contact with after resettlement. Educators, counsellors, administrators, and all school personnel need basic training on how to recognize trauma, how best to respond to trauma, and how to provide trauma-informed care. Without proper training, inappropriate or harmful responses may put children at risk for re-traumatization, or signs and symptoms of trauma may be overlooked, leaving children bereft of the necessary care. Educators also need to understand how trauma affects the child and how it impacts their social, academic, and psychological development. A child may respond with misbehaviour, withdrawal, or disassociation and without consideration for the reasons behind the behaviour, children may be unfairly disciplined or simply ignored. Many school discipline policies and zero-tolerance models do not take into account the issues that many children are struggling with, and this can be both harmful and hurtful (McCluskey & McCluskey, 2001).

Children will talk to people they trust and respect. As our research revealed, this person is often a member of the school community. It may be a custodian, a teacher, a coach, or the front desk staff. All school staff need to be prepared to respond, refer, and recommend strategies to support these students (Stewart, 2017b). As our research also revealed, the person a child chooses to talk to may in some cases be the only trusted adult in a child's life; therefore, it is imperative that the entire school community be equipped with the knowledge and skills to respond appropriately.

CULTURAL BROKERS IN EDUCATION AND CAREER DEVELOPMENT

Confusion, uncertainty, and doubt can flood newcomers to a country as they struggle to learn about acceptable practices, laws, social norms, morals, customs, and the general habits of a new society. These feelings compound the uncertainty, fear, apprehension, and losses (routine, identity, stability) experienced by those who have been forcibly displaced from their homelands and relocated to host countries. The realization that the way things were done in the country of origin differ, sometimes drastically, from the way things are done in the new country of migration, may lead to culture shock. The unique and timely assistance of a cultural broker can mitigate this shock and ease the transition.

Cultural brokering involves transitional support that bridges or mediates between people of different cultural groups or backgrounds in order to reduce conflict or affect change (Jezewski, 1990, in *National Center for Cultural Competency* [NCCC], 2004, p. vii). It has been recognized historically across many disciplines, including health, settlement, and education, in multiple countries. The cultural broker enables the transfer of ideas, beliefs, and underlying assumptions between both parties through effective cross-cultural communication, including the cultural nuances of both verbal and non-verbal communication (NCCC, 2004). Just as translation permits communication between speakers of different languages, cultural brokering facilitates understanding between people from different cultures.

According to Yohani (2010, p. 7), cultural brokers in education ease communication between school personnel and students from different cultural groups in a way that allows students and their families to discuss their differences and similarities with the school in an effort to learn from one another. In this context, the cultural broker clarifies cultural experiences and differences to teachers, parents, and students in meaningful, culturally safe ways. An educational cultural broker may do something as simple as translating or interpreting for parents, students, and teachers, or as complex as helping newcomer youth determine their future career path.

Involving cultural brokers in the education and career development of newcomer youth can reduce potential barriers in the educational setting. These may exist at multiple levels, such as the educational setting itself, specific learning environments, assumptions about previous learning experiences, unfamiliar teaching techniques and learning expectations, and even the ascribed roles of educators and students.

In some cultures, the family holds the greatest power in the education of a child, and gender plays a role in the educational opportunities afforded each child. In other cultures, it is the teacher who is perceived as the ultimate unquestionable authority. The culture of a country of origin, and of its educational milieu, influences how refugee and newcomer youth adapt to and participate in the educational system of a new country. A cultural broker acting as a liaison helps create positive relationships between parents, students, teachers, and counsellors that increase opportunities for student success.

Cultural brokers can help those working in the school system to effectively address gaps in knowledge that may impede teaching and learning. This is due to their unique awareness of the culture, language, and specific needs of students with refugee or newcomer backgrounds—needs that are often unknown to both educators and families and are unique to each family, based on the journey from their place of origin to the community in which they have been welcomed. Currently, pre-service teachers in Canada are not formally taught how to be culturally responsive to, and inclusive of, refugee and newcomer students. Furthermore, the cultural and linguistic diversity of newcomer populations makes it difficult for educators to prepare sufficiently for all of the children that arrive in their schools and classrooms. Cultural brokers who are aware of racial, ethnic, linguistic, and cultural components of both the receiving institution and the newcomer's place of origin are able to facilitate smoother integration.

Educational cultural brokers are neutral, culturally informed, and speak the language of educators. They can increase opportunities for inclusion and help create transitional support. The result is a more informed, collaborative environment for learning which benefits all learners, their families, and educators.

CHARACTERISTICS OF CULTURAL BROKERS

Ideally, cultural brokers possess linguistic and cultural competency, are trusted and respected by their community, and show some sort of credibility or relatedness to the cultures they are working with, such as being a newcomer and having experience in a newcomer setting. The broker should have knowledge of the languages, values, beliefs, and practices of both the host country and the country of origin. While sharing the same language and culture helps in cultural brokering, researchers argue that it is sufficient for the broker to be culturally sensitive and have a keen awareness of cultural needs.

EDUCATIONAL CULTURAL BROKERS IN CANADA

Who and where are the educational cultural brokers in Canada? In some communities, a community member becomes an informal cultural broker, by virtue of his or her background, experience, and skills. Some schools have cultural brokers in the form of cultural support works or liaison officers. In other schools, the role of cultural broker is assumed by one or more staff members or others. Teachers, counsellors, peers, in-school settlement service provides, fellow students, past students, translators, or social workers can all serve as cultural brokers.

The literature around educational cultural brokering within the population of newcomer youth in Canada focuses on

- the psychological well-being of newcomer youth (Brar, 2010),
- the multicultural counselling competencies for school counsellors (Brar-Josan & Yohani, 2014), and
- the opportunities and challenges for newcomer students (Yohani, 2010).

The role of cultural broker spans both micro and macro levels of integration. At the micro level, brokers assist in the day-to-day processes of facilitating school adaptation for students, offering supportive counselling, and bridging children and parents to services (Brar, 2010). Brokers also provide essential conflict-resolution and mediation services between and among parents, schools, students, and others. Early intervention and remediation can mitigate many potential or emerging problems, some of which may be unforeseen by the newcomers. A broker's interactions and support can also act as a protective "shield" for both the newcomers and the community, adding to levels of resiliency. At the macro level, because systems are slower to adjust to change, the educational cultural broker offers an element of advocacy and awareness in the larger educational and social community that expedites the transformation of the system, allowing for more open and flexible opportunities to accommodate diversity (Brar, 2010).

Of course, educational cultural brokers can support educational systems, refugee/newcomer students, and their families both informally and formally. Informally, brokers can facilitate cultural integration and increase a sense of belonging, two issues that strongly contribute to the educational well-being and integration of youth (Brar, 2010). In terms of career development, post-secondary options, and potential employment, brokers, together with school counsellors, may also help youth connect to bridging settlement services. Additionally, cultural brokers often assist youth and/or their parents with finances and housing to mitigate additional barriers to smooth and efficient social, economic, and cultural integration. Furthermore, brokers who are well-connected to school systems and the community may provide encouragement and additional emotional support, guidance, and information for youth investigating their plans beyond school, and may help them to navigate parent–youth relationships. Formally, brokers provide contextual information and cultural interpretations that assist with referrals and ongoing education, training, and employment opportunities.

CHALLENGES FOR EDUCATIONAL CULTURAL BROKERS

The role of an educational cultural broker is sometimes ambiguous; this ambiguity may pose as a challenge, especially when sensitive issues are involved. Yohani (2010) stresses the need for broker in educational and cultural settings to have a clearly defined role. Working in a consultative and collaborative manner avoids potential conflicts when the broker's role overlaps with the responsibilities of other professionals and agencies. When this happens, consultation and collaboration among those involved can help avoid conflicts.

Another potential risk emerges if a student and broker come from the same ethno-cultural community, a situation with the potential for vicarious trauma and other stress-related conditions (Yohani, 2010).

Ethical conflicts and legal conundrums are also prevalent in the work of a cultural broker. The following example of a high-risk situation helps to illustrate this challenge. An educational cultural broker may be assisting both the student and his or her family. The newly arrived family is dependent on provincial financial assistance, and the cultural broker knows that a member of the family is working. As per Canadian law, if someone in the family is working and earning above a certain amount of money per month, there is an obligation to notify the provincial financial assistance agency. A cultural broker would clearly be in a conflicted situation if the student or the family requested non-disclosure. The broker, as a professional working in the best interest of the family, is in a precarious situation—not wanting to damage a productive relationship while simultaneously needing to inform the family of the need to adhere to the law.

Advocating on behalf of parents or students sometimes requires great sensitivity. The case of one cultural broker working with a family who had one child of each gender, two years apart, is illustrative. When both children were in middle school, integration and inclusion at school were smooth; however, when the female child was promoted to high school in a different school building, her father refused to send her to school since her brother would not be with her as he had been in middle school. The cultural broker in this case needed to explain with great care how the father could uphold his cultural and religious beliefs while allowing his daughter to continue her education, despite her brother's absence.

Another example involves the use of force in correcting child behaviour. Cultural norms and laws differ from one country to another; refugee and newcomer families are often not aware of these differences and often hold to practices they know from their family of origin in their country of origin. One cultural broker tells of being placed in the difficult position of explaining to a parent that corporal punishment is not tolerated in Canada, and that as a parent, there would be legal, punitive consequences for such behaviour. The response from the parent unfamiliar with Canada was culturally quite understandable: "but this is my house, and in my house I can do whatever I want." The culture of childrearing in Canada is often quite invisible and therefore likely unknown by newcomers. As this cultural broker indicated, there is an increased need for culturally responsive positive parenting in Canada. Programs that teach such skills exist in major cities and are attracting interested parents who truly care about the well-being of their children. However, the number of programs is very low compared to the size of newly arriving populations, and attendance by newly arrived families at these parenting programs is also nominal. One reason for this discrepancy relates to the social determinants of health: fulfilling the family's basic needs takes priority over parenting and parenting classes. Another reason is an absence of information about parenting in Canada for refugee and newcomer families and the difficulties in finding childcare to allow parents to attend the programs. Information and programs may both be lacking in some geographic areas of settlement.

CHALLENGES AND RISKS FOR EDUCATIONAL CULTURAL BROKERS

- Potential conflict when responsibilities overlap with those of other professionals
- Vicarious trauma
- Ethical conflicts and sensitive situations
- Inadequate information and/or training on stress and mental health issues

Cultural brokers are well-positioned to notice signs and symptoms of stress and mental health issues within newcomer families. This already challenging role is made more difficult if brokers do not have adequate information and training on prevalent mental health concerns. Frequently, refugee youth build trust in cultural brokers and may be more comfortable conveying information to the broker rather than to a parent who they fear might judge them, or a teacher who may lack facility in the youth's primary language or understanding of his/her culture. Building on that trust, brokers require education in mental health issues so they can appropriately probe for mental health concerns and refer individuals and their families to appropriate professionals and services in a culturally sensitive manner.

THE ROLE OF LANGUAGE IN CULTURALLY RESPONSIVE EDUCATION

In a country with two official languages and a history of encouraging immersion programs in schools, as well as countless Indigenous and heritage languages, it would be easy to assume that language acquisition for refugee and newcomer children and youth in Canadian schools is a simple feat. Perspectives from across Canada do not find this assumption to be true. Research measuring educational success when English or French is not the first language clearly indicates that the amount of formal schooling students have received in their first language is the primary indicator of success in learning an additional language (Thomas & Collier, 1997), and there is a strong suggestion from language acquisition scholars that "monolingually-normed approaches to pedagogy and assessment with linguistically diverse student populations in North America are detrimental to their academic achievement" (Ricento, 2013, p. 349).

What does this mean for best practices in the classroom for refugee and newcomer children and youth, who often have interrupted education, minimal formal language instruction, and do not speak either official language of Canada? Key concepts related to the intersection of literacy, academics, language, and culture are conducive to positive educational experiences in culturally responsible classrooms.

Effectively learning an additional language depends upon the learner having literacy skills in another language but also the ability to transfer knowledge and awareness of that language, culture, and experience—including the links between oral and written language—to the new language, culture, and experience. When students have had limited formal education or limited access to their first language or literacy due to transitory lifestyles, crises, disability, or unavailability of linguistic resources (e.g., practice with oral language, hearing the language, reading materials), they require more intensive instruction before they can enter a classroom designed for English/French as an additional language and succeed.

When students have established literacy skills in their first language, they are better able to understand the mechanics of the new language and its relationship to the life experiences and culture of the new country. According to Ricento (2013, p. 358), the best predictor of academic success in a second language is the number of years of schooling in the first language. Ricento also indicates that there are negative implications on the acquisition of academic English that directly correlate with immersion into mainstream English classes (p. 356). One can assume that the same would be true for French-language immersion in a French-dominant society. These findings imply that simultaneously trying to learn a language, academic subject matter, and social norms is too great a task for most learners.

Culturally responsive education requires school systems to recognize the primary needs of refugee and newcomer children and youth before immersing them into the full educational experience. Referring back to figure 1 (p. 24), Stewart (2011) identified six primary basic challenges that refugees reported as being the foundation for all others: food, clothing, safety, shelter, power, and belonging. These core challenges are the first level of adjustment for newcomers and refugees who are forcibly displaced from their homes. All too often, the struggle to satisfy these basic human needs becomes a long-term battle.

Preparing students for a new environment, a new system of learning, a new language, and a new culture is key to their success and allows for a smooth transition into the regular classroom. Including students in the school's social, cultural, and athletic life creates an important bridge to full inclusion in the linguistic and cultural complexity of the regular classroom and Canadian education system.

Culturally responsive education is not a one-way street, in which adjustments are made only for the refugee and newcomer students. Culturally responsive education aims to increase awareness of, and encourage, diversity and positive perspective-taking among all students. Learning outcomes to that effect already exist in mandatory curricula focused on diversity. Regular classrooms hosting both Canadian-born, native speakers and non-Canadian born, alternate language speakers offer a rich learning environment that encourages the development of cultural competency and global citizenship for all students.

Perhaps one of the most important concepts that Ricento (2013) articulates relates to fair assessment processes for newcomer children and youth. Any student arriving in Canada and entering the Canadian school system must be assessed based on their individual trajectory and using multiple measures, since many language assessments are culturally bound and mono-linguistically formulated. He suggests that the benefits of being bilingual or multilingual are often absent from assessment measures. Further, many K–12 schools do not recognise or value the speaking and writing of "other" languages in considering ways to enhance student performance (pp. 363–364).

Canada is home to people from multiple countries of origin, and its school systems must offer all students education in the skills and knowledge necessary to positively interact and communicate with the many cultural and linguistic groups that live and work here. The *Blueprint for Life/Work Designs* (see Section Three) supports students' positive self-identity and career development in a diverse, rapidly changing world. With added cultural knowledge and value-added learning opportunities for refugee and newcomer students in their classrooms, intercultural and global citizenship becomes a reality for all.

● ● ● ●

ADAPTING SCHOOL-WIDE PBIS TO THE EXPERIENCES OF REFUGEE AND NEWCOMER STUDENTS

Teachers are quite familiar with the work of Terrance Scott and knowledgeable about implementing a continuum of school-wide positive behaviour interventions and supports PBIS (Newfoundland and Labrador Department of Education and Early Childhood Development, n.d.). In the case of students whose backgrounds include newcomer status, refugee experiences, potential trauma, and interrupted education, particularly because of war and violent uprisings, the continuum can be adapted to begin to provide culturally safe and appropriate supports in the educational setting.

TRAUMA-INFORMED CARE VALUES

Five key values form a solid foundation for trauma-informed care: safety, empowerment, collaboration, trust, and choice (Fallot & Harris, 2001). Whether educators are working with full classrooms of diverse students (Tier 1 supports and interventions), small groups of students who require more directed learning (Tier 2 supports and interventions), or individual students who require unique supports specific to their learning needs (Tier 3 supports and interventions), the foundation is the same (see figure 2). Regardless of the cognitive abilities of students, a sense of safety and trust are essential to learning. If these two fundamental human needs are not addressed, students will remain in the fight/freeze/flight stage and little substantive learning can take place. Only once students feel a sense of safety and trust can they entertain the notion of "belonging," and with belonging comes collaboration, empowerment, and choice. Particularly for vulnerable students, students with interrupted education, and students who are newcomers or from war affected areas, it is these five "care values" that form the foundation for all potential learning and growing.

Figure 2. Three tiers of positive behaviour interventions and supports (PBIS)

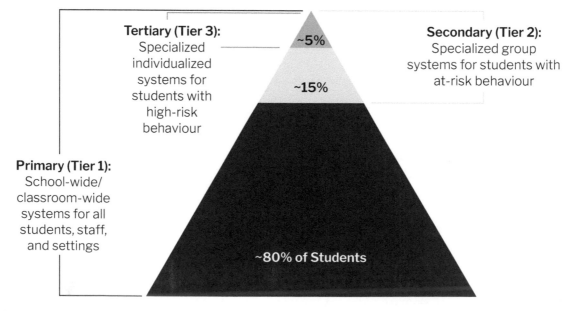

(Adapted from http://www.pbis.org)

PROVIDING SUPPORT

Educators are typically well-versed in supporting students in the area of academics. It is, after all, the focus of most of their training. They also have education and training in behavioural supports and cognitive skills, though teacher education, whether pre-service or in-service, tends to address behavioural supports and cognitive skills in generic areas related to discipline, differentiated instruction, and inclusive education. It is rare for educators to learn specific information or strategies related to the unique needs of vulnerable populations such as refugee and newcomer students. For this reason, ongoing professional development is often required to address the teaching and learning needs of students who have difficulties with emotional and psychological regulation, or who have difficulties transitioning to a new environment, culture, or climate. Fair assessment practices and screening for such students requires a collaborative–consultative approach with community partners, and parent/caregiver involvement. Increasing educators' capacity to anticipate and respond to the needs of refugee and newcomer students creates opportunities for crisis prevention and social–emotional learning.

The life and educational experiences of students are diverse and complex. When educators and support personnel can recognize and respond to underlying factors that facilitate or impede progress, opportunities for success increase. There are some factors to keep in mind when providing support.

- **Recognize that behaviour is typically the first sign of an underlying concern.** When language fails, when sense of self or community is weakened, when resiliency is low, determining what a student's behaviour is trying to communicate is key.
- **Respect the individual and his/her journey.** Recognize that students are individuals and each is involved in major life transitions that include personal growth and development, new environments, new cultures, and new expectations.
- **Begin at the beginning.** Teach students about common situations that may arise and how to respond to those situations. If appropriate responses to typical situations continue to be absent, determine whether the starting point was developmentally, socially, and culturally aligned with the student.
- **Be flexible**—in planning, in approaching topics, in building relationships. All good teaching and learning begins and ends with relationships and alliances. Celebrate successes, accept the underlying reasons for current behaviours and attitudes.
- **Ask for assistance.** Let the student guide you in determining what is needed for success. Check with the family of the student, community helpers knowledgeable about refugee and newcomer experience, your professional peers, and support staff.

• • • •

CREATING A CARING COMMUNITY

The following tips were originally published in Manitoba School Counsellor magazine (Stewart, 2016). Each section—Connect, Accept, Refer, and Emotional Expression—describes principles and actions for creating a community of care and compassion, in classrooms and school-wide. See also Guiding Principles for Supporting Newcomer and Refugee Students (Appendix, pp. 221-222).

CONNECT

Connect with children and their families, connect students, to other students and connect staff to students.

Don't worry about language. If the student or their family does not speak or does not have understanding of English, don't panic. Your non-verbal actions will say more than words. Smile, offer open and friendly gestures, look approachable and children/youth will know they are welcome. Translate school information and letters into different languages so that parents know what is happening in the school and so they feel acknowledged and accepted. Parents may not feel they are welcome in the school or they may be working or tending to children and coming to school may not be possible. Sometimes children will naturally gravitate to someone in the school who they feel is safe and accepting. This could be a teacher, a coach, a counsellor, an administrator, a custodian, or an office assistant. All staff and students have a role to play in connecting newcomers to your school environment. Provide opportunities for other students to meet newcomer students. Sports, music, drama, art, cooking, gardening, whatever it is, provide a variety of opportunities for students to connect with each other both inside and outside of class. Offer up your own talents and gifts and start a club in the school to forge connections that might not normally occur. Reaching out and connecting students to each other is the most effective way to prevent discrimination and racism.

ACCEPT

Accept difference, foster culturally responsive schools, and provide a safe environment to learn about diversity.

Provide a safe environment in your classrooms and schools where students can ask questions about cultural differences and where they can look for and identify injustices and inequality. Accept everyone and keep your expectations high for all students. No one rises to low expectations. Know how your own cultural lens informs your teaching and interactions with others. Accept that students who have come from refugee backgrounds will have diverse histories and could have had very traumatic or disrupted experiences that may seriously affect their ability to feel safe or accepted in school. Accept that it will be nearly impossible to teach someone who is feeling threatened or unsafe in your classroom. It will take time to build trust. Allow time for the student to feel safe in your classroom by establishing routines and consistency. Some newcomers may have had limited or no schooling prior to arriving in your classroom. Accept that they are in your class now and it is your responsibility to provide the most supportive and accommodating environment to them.

REFER

It is ok not to know what to do or to feel incapable of supporting children. You cannot be everything to everyone.

There are instances when a student may have experienced such horrific events that he or she will need more than you can offer as a teacher. There may also be multidimensional issues that are far beyond your level of expertise. Know who can support you in the school and community. Know who you can reach out to for additional help. Keep a list of community agencies, settlement services, psychosocial support workers, youth organizations, or teacher networks who can assist you. Do not feel isolated and do not think you need to do this alone. If you contact someone and they do not help, try another person until you find someone who will help. Work together and collaborate with others who are committed to assisting children and who are willing to work to solve problems with creative solutions. It is common for refugee students to have many interrelated and intersecting challenges concerning education, housing, health, employment, and settlement. Rarely do issues occur in only one system. Work together, share information, and rely on them when you need assistance and be there when they also need you.

EMOTIONAL EXPRESSION

Help students learn how to express themselves in a healthy and helpful way. Develop your own skills to maintain work life balance and keep a hopeful and helpful perspective.

Help foster positive coping skills such as stress management, relaxation, mindfulness, and expression of anger. Students may need guidance and support to help them work through feelings of anger from being displaced or from experiencing violence. Smells, sounds, or people could trigger a very unwanted feeling of anxiety or stress. Students with refugee backgrounds may run or panic when they are in a difficult state. Western techniques may not work with students from other parts of the world. Music, dance, drama, drumming, coloring, drawing, or physical activity may be more therapeutic or helpful as opposed to one-to-one meetings or group discussions. Be open to new techniques. Develop your own strategies for keeping calm and maintaining a positive outlook. Anticipate setbacks, see them as challenges and maintain a hopeful attitude.

1

ADDRESSING THE NEEDS OF REFUGEE AND NEWCOMER CHILDREN

Taken together, recent research into the needs of refugee and newcomer children in Canada, provides an emerging sense of the ecological environment and its attendant challenges. The participants in our study pointed out educational, environmental, and psychosocial challenges that can often spiral out of control towards the failure of some students to find success in their new country. Initiatives to address these challenges provided by participants in our study are consistent with those of a 2011 study undertaken by Jan Stewart. Tables 4 and 5 consolidate recommendations provided by students, parents, educators, counsellors, administrators, consultants, and liaison workers in the 2011 study.

Fortunately, a preponderance of these recommendations can be found in existing curriculum and implementation documents for educators in many provinces and territories. The structures in which they are found (e.g., teaching strategies, lesson plans) are easily adapted for refugee and newcomer children in schools and simultaneously cover grade-level learning outcomes for all learners. Educators are not required to teach "more content"; rather, they are required to teach "more context" when their classrooms hold diverse learners with diverse instructional needs. Health Education, Social Studies, English Language Arts, and comprehensive guidance and counselling programs are the primary areas in which existing learning outcomes address the needs of refugee and newcomer children. Additionally, many ministries of education across Canada have developed guides for teaching students who require supports related to English or French as an additional language, special education, and differentiated education.

Tables 4 and 5 list multiple initiatives related to the intersection of economic, environmental, educational, and psychosocial challenges. In many schools across Canada, these initiatives may be sporadically or informally implemented. In a smaller number of schools that regularly receive refugee and newcomer students, many of these initiatives are well established and part of the culture of the school. To adequately address the needs of an increasing number of refugee and newcomer children and youth, these initiatives must become far more prominent in the daily activities of school life. Educators are best able to provide effective, timely supports when initiatives related to education, environment, and psychosocial needs are part of the regular activities of the school day.

Table 4. Initiatives to address educational and environmental challenges

Educational challenges	Environmental challenges
Provide opportunities for mentoring.	Implement more community and school partnerships.
Provide academic and vocational tutoring.	Provide more liaison workers.
Coordinate a re-entry program to help bring students back to school after they have dropped out.	Designate specific teachers as case managers who provide links to the ecological systems.
Teach pre-service courses in EAL strategies for all teachers and on refugee issues.	Designate a person who is able to advocate for the student.
Coordinate provincial and division policy development.	Implement multi-agency partnering on projects (justice and education, and non-government agencies, immigration).
Conduct leadership seminars on teaching in multi-ethnic cities and on utilizing community sources and resources.	Coordinate a sustained and intensive anti-racism and discrimination campaign in the school, community, private sector, and public services.
Acknowledge foreign-based professional programs.	Provide information for newcomers in video format in several languages.
Set up a school-based resource site that links to agencies.	Develop parent modules for helping children through school and for identifying signs of trouble.
Teach basic skills and social development.	Provide more student-to-student assistance.
Offer scholarships and bursaries to encourage involvement in sport.	Create and implement a culturally and linguistically appropriate assessment process.
Teach career development and awareness programs for all students.	
Train immigrant and refugee students to be mediators and peer counsellors.	
Provide training and education for refugee parents on issues related to discipline, personal safety, and adolescent development.	

(Stewart, 2011, Table 5.2)

Table 5. Initiatives to address economic and psychosocial challenges

Economic challenges	Psychosocial challenges
Build in an incentive program for staying in school, so students do not have to work full-time.	Provide more preventative programming.
Prepare students for independent living.	Provide group support programs to assist with the integration of the person with the community.
Provide more information on work skills and employee rights.	Implement initial screening and ongoing screening to identify psychosocial challenges.
Provide volunteer placement programs for refugee students who transition to job placements.	Provide arts-based activities (film, play, theatre, videography, dance) in school and the community.
Teach EAL programs for parents outside of school hours.	Train clinical staff on issues related to refugees.
Utilize technology-based communication and support.	Implement language and literacy programs that include trained professionals who know how to recognize and respond to psychosocial issues.
Remove government loan for the cost of airfare from country of origin.	Provide integrated emotional, spiritual, and health care.
	Train all students in conflict prevention.

(Stewart, 2011, Table 5.3)

● ● ● ●

RECOMMENDATIONS EMERGING FROM OUR RESEARCH

Focus group consultations in each province resulted in many recommendations for best practices to meet the career and life development needs of newcomer and refugee youth. The best practices have been organized according to 13 overarching themes. The best practices intersect at many points with recommendations for policies to address the challenges faced by newcomers and refugees (see Recommended Policies, below). Together, these practices and policies provide the foundation for the teacher lessons and student activities that follow in Sections 2 and 3 of this guide.

BEST PRACTICES

1. A Holistic Approach

Schools should engage with the families and communities of their students. If possible, teachers should pay home visits to students who continue to have challenges at school, and establish partnerships with supporting agencies to do family work. Schools should help newcomer parents to understand the norms and expectations of the Canadian school system, Canadian workplaces, and Canadian citizenship. Schools should also have regular field trips to settlement service providers and community support services with the objective to expand the support networks for students. The community should be able to funnel information to teachers and mentors.

2. Support Workers in Schools

Schools that have a certain proportion of students with higher needs should have family therapists, grief counsellors, resource teachers, community support workers, and social workers. Provincial funding should be made available to hire cultural brokers. These schools should also have student representatives to help advocate for students and their families.

3. Schools as Community Hubs

Schools with high percentages (30–50%) of E/FAL students should receive additional funding for extracurricular and co-curricular activities. After-school classes should be provided for E/FAL students in particular. Schools should serve as community hubs with after-school programs, language classes, and community programs to help newcomers adjust and succeed. Programs should be accessible to everyone.

4. Transition Centres

Each school division should have a transition centre for newcomer children and families. Centre staff should be educated on the needs of refugee students and the needs of staff working with them. Centres can provide alternate learning options (transitional schooling) for students who have had interrupted learning. Centres can also provide extra transitional support to newcomer families after their first year, when financial support stops.

5. Evaluating Student Growth

Students' progress should be evaluated from a holistic perspective and not just through grades. This may require adjusting learning outcomes and overall academic structures. Schools should meet students' needs instead of compelling students to meet school demands. Middle school and high school teachers should be available during the school day to answer students' questions about a particular subject or class.

6. The Physical Classroom Environment

The number of students in E/FAL classes—or in classes with large numbers of E/FAL students—should be small. The classroom environment (furniture, lighting, floor plan) should be meticulously planned and spacious.

7. Career Development

High school students should have access to programs that can connect them to the world of work and to further education or training. Life/career education should become a curricular priority and should be infused across all subject areas.

8. Self-Care

Mandatory classes/teaching on healthy lifestyles (e.g., nutrition, sport, social activity) should be incorporated into the school year for all students and teachers. This should include sessions on self-care and mindfulness practices at school.

9. Professional Development

Teachers (including pre-service teachers) and staff should receive continuing cultural competency training. Educators should also receive training on trauma-informed perspectives, teaching war affected children and youth, mental health, and basic counselling skills. Staff should have the opportunity to get professional development from service providers, thus building connections with them and getting access to their resources.

10. Teacher Education

All education students should be required to take 3-hour credit courses on teaching E/FAL students and supporting newcomer students. Cultural competency, basic counselling skills, and trauma-informed care should also be mandatory topics in their training. Students should have the option of pursuing a Bachelor of Education degree with E/FAL as a teachable or an undergraduate degree in E/FAL. Universities should also offer a post-baccalaureate program or certification in teaching E/FAL students.

11. Employment Policies

Diversity in the work force should be emphasized. Newcomers should be given the opportunity to work as teachers, educational assistants, and general employees of school divisions. There should be equal pay for all educational assistants.

12. Funding

Health, housing, and education should be funded together to foster wraparound services. More investment is particularly needed for mental health services and resources, and for pre-arrival programming and services. Resources for newcomers should not be segregated based on nationality.

13. National and Provincial Collaborations

There is a need to develop directories of programs, services, and agencies serving newcomers and refugees. Directories should be accessible to all relevant systems (health, education, justice, early childhood, workplace agencies, post-secondary education, housing, and settlement). Schools should receive information on government-funded resources within their vicinities so that they can access what they need and identify collaborators and partners. Provincial governments should facilitate multi-agency collaboration and partnerships, provincially and nationally.

RECOMMENDED POLICIES

For initiatives that support the success of all learners to be aligned and effective, policies related to the education and well-being of refugee and newcomer children, youth, and their families must be mandated. Our national, qualitative research with a range of participants—teacher-educators, students, parents, counsellors, administrators, consultants, and liaison workers—produced a series of potential policies for governments to consider. The policies are listed in table 6.

These initiatives and potential policies to address the needs of refugee and newcomer students reflect a distillation of the theoretical knowledge and practical implementation experiences of educators and policy-makers across Canada. As previously outlined, pre-existing documents address many of the recommendations of study participants. Professional competency, curriculum, and support documents, combined with implementation guides, are a rich source of assistance to educators in differentiating instruction and learning based on the unique needs of all students, including those who are refugees and newcomers to Canada.

Many of the recommendations from our study are founded on an urgent desire to make learning accessible and contextualized, related to real-world experiences of life and work in Canada, and focused on strategies that increase the self-knowledge of the learner. This foundation is fundamental to all teaching and learning in classrooms across Canada, regardless of student demographics.

Table 6. Recommended policies to address educational, environmental, and psychosocial challenges

Jurisdiction	Rationale	Recommended policy
Federal	There is insufficient funding in provincial/territorial budgets for the work required to successfully integrate federally-sponsored refugees and immigrants into local communities.	The federal government shall provide protected transfer funding to provinces/ territories commensurate with migration patterns, to support specified emergency conditions and evidence-based programs that address the successful integration of refugees and immigrants to Canada.
Provincial / Territorial	Increased collaboration and interdepartmental funding are urgently needed to support effective wraparound care for immigrants and refugees.	Interdepartmental funding (health, families, education) shall be provided to facilitate wraparound services for immigrants and refugees in these areas • Housing • Adult E/FAL • Special services • Education • Mental health/health services
	Provincial funding for evidence-based educational practices and resources must keep pace with the volume, intensity, and frequency of immigrant and refugee needs during the newcomer time period.	Each school division shall receive funding based on provincial funding formulas for culturally safe transition centres for newcomer children and their families.
	Ministries of education have a unique opportunity to support schools in the delivery of effective, culturally safe programming.	Ministries of education shall undertake a pan-Canadian protocol related to newcomer education and resource sharing.
	Ministries of education have a unique opportunity to equalize access to school programs.	Ministries of education shall develop and distribute to schools standardized intake assessment tools for newcomer students.
	There is a need for accessible and user-friendly provincial/territorial directories of all services for newcomers, to be used by educational institutions, families, and government/community agencies.	Ministries of families shall undertake a pan-Canadian initiative to collate and regularly update a pan-Canadian directory of government-funded resources for newcomers that is organized by province/territory and includes a glossary of terms and standardized acronyms.

Jurisdiction	Rationale	Recommended policy
Municipal	Newcomer refugee and immigrant youth and families lack the economic ability to travel by public transportation to learning centres, medical care, employment, and schooling.	Local governments in major centres with public transportation shall provide time-limited bus passes at no cost to youth and families identified as immigrant or refugee newcomers.
Teacher training institutions	Teacher-training institutions play an important role in educating future teachers on the increasing needs of newcomer learners in Canadian schools.	Degrees in education shall provide students with the option of pursuing E/FAL as a teachable area at the Bachelor level and cross-discipline E/FAL programs at the post-baccalaureate level.
School boards	Schools need to increase capacity for addressing students with E/FAL backgrounds.	Schools shall provide E/FAL professional learning opportunities for teachers and para-professionals who do not have qualifications in the area of additional languages.
	Community school–based extra-curricular activities to connect immigrant and refugee newcomers assist in successful integration and adjustment.	School divisions shall provide additional funding for after-school programs, language classes, and culturally safe community programs to those schools within their catchment area with populations of E/FAL students in the range of 30% to 50%.
Schools	Diversity in the workforce assists in cultural safety.	Schools shall consider diversity in their hiring practices with particular attention to newcomers.
	Fair assessment processes assist in strategic and appropriate student placement and a sense of inclusion.	Schools shall have policies that require appropriately qualified staff members to conduct language testing and assess school readiness for newcomer and refugee students.
	Appropriate and ongoing training in the workforce assists in student and staff effectiveness and safety.	Schools shall require regular staff training in culturally safe and trauma-informed teaching practices.

SECTION TWO

BUILDING COMPETENCY IN EDUCATORS

• • • • •

Know yourself. Know your audience.

All lessons related to refugee and newcomer experiences require educator mindfulness.

Be aware of unintended consequences, particularly when teaching vulnerable populations.

Be alert for, attuned to, and aware of the signs and symptoms of personal and participant distress.

INTRODUCTION

The *Canadian Standards and Guidelines for Career Development Practitioners (Standards and Guidelines)* outlines the core competencies that contribute to effective teaching of learning outcomes related to career development. The *Standards and Guidelines* offer a robust competency profile for professionals seeking to provide forward-thinking, life-affirming, career development services.

Three of the competency areas in particular support the needs of school counsellors and educators who are incorporating career development into their daily activities and who are working with newcomer and refugee students. These three areas highlight the intersection of self- and community-knowledge with student needs and their unique life experiences. The three areas are

- **C2 Interpersonal Competence** (including respecting diversity, communicating effectively, and developing productive interactions)
- **C3 Career Development Knowledge**
- **C4 Needs Assessment and Referral**

The following tables describe the relevant outcomes in these areas. Teachers who hold these competencies will combine them with their professional pedagogical skills, their knowledge of human development, and theories of learning to create rich and rewarding classroom experiences for all learners.

This section also includes 30 teacher lesson plans to help classroom teachers and school counsellors hone their skills and develop competency in these areas. The lessons are designed to be used by counsellor- and teacher-educators in various setting (e.g., workshops, professional development days).

CORE COMPETENCIES RELATED TO NEWCOMER AND REFUGEE CHILDREN IN CANADA

C2 Interpersonal Competence

C2.1 Respect Diversity		Related Teacher Lesson Plan
Demonstrate awareness and knowledge about diversity (C2.1.1)	• Describe the multiple influences of diversity, including client's characteristics and beliefs that are relevant to their career issues, work and environment contexts • Describe how client characteristics and beliefs and work and environment context can interact	6: Local Resources and Supports 9: Scaffolding Academic Learning for Additional Language Learners 10: Refugee Narratives and Case Studies 11: Refugee Case Studies 12: Academic Culture Shock 13: Cultural Tokenism Versus Diversity 14: Interrupted Learning 17: How Diverse Is Your World? 18: Defining and Understanding Culture
Demonstrate respect for diversity with all clients (C2.1.2)	• Be sensitive to the intra- and interpersonal dynamics of people from diverse populations • Respond to the career development needs unique to individuals of diverse populations • Access appropriate methods or resources to communicate with clients with specific needs	

C2.1 Respect Diversity		Related Teacher Lesson Plan
	• Work with colleagues, other professionals and community members including individuals from diverse backgrounds • Recognize and manage areas with respect to diversity in which they may carry assumption, are personally uncomfortable, or lack sufficient knowledge	22: Reflective and Meditative Painting as a Form of Stress Reduction 25: Matching Needs to Services 26: Understanding Loss and Grief 27: Trauma 30: Building Self-Resiliency

C2.2 Communicate Effectively		Related Teacher Lesson Plan
Use effective listening skills (C2.2.4)	• Use listening skills • Use reflecting skills • Use summarizing skills • Use prompts and leads	1: Peace and Conflict 2: Crisis in Syria 7: Restorative Practices in the Classroom 8: Privilege Walk 11: Refugee Case Studies 19: Basic Counselling Skill – Active Listening 20: Basic Counselling Skill – Attending 23: Basic Counselling Skill – Building Empathy 24: Artifact Storytelling 26: Understanding Loss and Grief
Clarify and provide feedback (C2.2.5)	• Support clients in self-assessing performance and behaviours • Provide descriptive and specific feedback on clients' performances or behaviours, when appropriate • Describe inconsistencies and ask clients to clarify them	
Establish and maintain collaborative work relationships (C2.2.6)	• Build rapport • Give other individuals their undivided attention • Establish the purpose of the relationship • Facilitate the exchange of information • Be sensitive to the needs and receptiveness of other individuals	

C2.3 Develop Productive Interactions with Clients		Related Teacher Lesson Plan
Foster client self-reliance and self-management (C2.3.1)	• Use a client-centred approach • Establish rapport • Educate clients about their own roles, responsibilities and choices in the career development process • Generate options with clients and offer choices • Guide clients' acquisition of the necessary attitudes, knowledge, and skills • Help clients to establish and commit to action plans	1: Peace and Conflict 2: Crisis in Syria 7: Restorative Practices in the Classroom 8: Privilege Walk 11: Refugee Case Studies 19: Basic Counselling Skill – Active Listening 20: Basic Counselling Skill – Attending 23: Basic Counselling Skill – Building Empathy 24: Artifact Storytelling 26: Understanding Loss and Grief
Deal with reluctant clients (C2.3.2)	• Conduct periodic review of action plans • Listen to clients • Determine sources of clients' reluctance • Inform clients of possible benefits of the process • Let clients know the option and potential results • Seek agreement on plans	

C3 Career Development Knowledge

C3.1 Possess Career Development Knowledge		Related Teacher Lesson Plan
Describe how human development models relate to career development (C3.1.1)	• Describe how common human development models may relate to career development (humanistic, behaviourist, developmental, etc.) • Describe human development models as they relate to your client groups, e.g., cognitive and emotional development of clients	5: Options for Post-Secondary Education 8: Privilege Walk 9: Scaffolding Academic Learning for Additional Language Learners 10: Refugee Narratives and Case Studies 16: Collaboration Between E/FAL and Subject-Area Teachers 25: Matching Needs to Services 28: Using Life Experiences to Direct Career Choices 29: Using Multiple Intelligences to Investigate Career Options
Describe how change and transition affect clients moving through the career process (C3.1.3)	• Describe types of change and transition • Recognize that change and transition are part of life • Recognize that the role of the career development practitioner is to help clients to learn to manage transitions and to guide clients through career-related changes	

C3.1 Possess Career Development Knowledge		Related Teacher Lesson Plan
	• Describe how models and theories can assist and encourage clients	5: Options for Post-Secondary Education
Describe how life roles and values impact career development (C3.1.4)	• Identify life roles and responsibilities that affect career development • Describe appropriate intervention options • Assist clients with the integration of career development within life roles	8: Privilege Walk 9: Scaffolding Academic Learning for Additional Language Learners 10: Refugee Narratives and Case Studies 16: Collaboration Between E/FAL and Subject-Area Teachers
Identity major components of the career planning process (C3.1.5)	• Identify the major components of the career planning process	25: Matching Needs to Services 28: Using Life Experiences to Direct Career Choices 29: Using Multiple Intelligences to Investigate Career Options
Identify the major organizations, resources and community-based services for career development (C3.1.6)	• Identify organizations, resources and community-based services relevant to their client groups • Know how to access information pertaining to organizations, resources, and services relevant to their client groups • Describe services offered by each organization	
Explain components of labour market information (C3.1.7)	• Access and explain components affecting the labour market • Possess an understanding of primary, secondary, and tertiary economies	
Keep current about the labour market (C3.1.8)	• Keep current about the community's labour market	
Keep current about diversity issues (C3.1.9)	• Be aware of the demographics of their community • Describe diversity issues in their community • Identify community resources/services available to diverse clients • Describe relevant legislation which may affect diverse clients	

C4 Needs Assessment and Referral

C4.1 Refer Clients to the Appropriate Sources		Related Teacher Lesson Plan
Respond to clients' needs (C4.1.1)	• Use a variety of methods and/or models to help clients identify their needs on an ongoing basis • Collaborate with clients to determine the most appropriate action to meet clients' needs • Initiate next steps with clients	5: Options for Post-Secondary Education 6: Local Resources and Supports 13: Cultural Tokenism Versus Diversity 16: Collaboration Between E/FAL and Subject-Area Teachers 17: How Diverse Is Your World?
Develop and maintain a referral network (C4.1.2)	• Access or organize an information system for referral sources • Liaise with others to exchange referral information about available and current resources • Establish community linkages between clients with special needs and community resources	
Make appropriate referrals (C4.1.3)	• Collaborate with clients to choose the most appropriate referrals • Assist clients as needed and appropriate • Complete all necessary documentation • Confirm with other agencies that referrals are appropriate • Follow-up on referrals	

● ● ● ●

LESSON PLANS TO BUILD TEACHER COMPETENCY

The following lesson plans are linked to competency areas in the *Standards and Guidelines* and themes identified in our research as being most relevant and helpful to working with refugee and newcomer children.

Each plan is divided into at least four parts: activation, acquisition, application, and assessment. An anticipatory set is sometimes included. Assessment ideas and tasks are informal and mostly formative.

TEACHER LESSON 1: PEACE AND CONFLICT

Objectives	Increase knowledge of current international conflicts and the importance of perspective-taking
Themes	**THEME 1:** Conflict Awareness **THEME 3:** Peace and Sustainability
Standards and Guidelines **Competency Areas**	C2.3: Develop Productive Interactions with Clients C2.2: Communicate Effectively
Materials	• *The Enemy: A Book about Peace* by Davide Cali, illustrated by Serge Bloch (New York: Schwartz & Wade, 2009): https://www.youtube.com/watch?v=x3K_iny61Ew • "Rwanda Genocide: 100 Days of Slaughter," BBC News, April 7, 2014: http://www.bbc.com/news/world-africa-26875506 • Venn Diagram (p. 53) • Pens/pencils

ANTICIPATORY SET:

- Ask participants to turn to a partner and discuss the following questions:
    - What causes war?
    - How do people become enemies?
    - Once a war has started, can it be stopped?
    - What role does propaganda have in fuelling hate that leads to war?

ACTIVATION:

- Ask participants to think about the following (there is no need to share):
    - Have you every believed something about someone based solely on what another person told you?
    - Have you ever been surprised because you expected a person to be one way and discovered that they were different?
    - Has there ever been a person that you didn't like at first but changed your mind about afterwards or over time? Maybe you even became friends.

ACQUISITION:

- Read *The Enemy: A Book about Peace* by Davide Cali.
  You can find a reading of the book at https://www.youtube.com/watch?v=x3K_iny61Ew.

2

APPLICATION:

- After reading/hearing *The Enemy*, consider the history of the 1994 Rwandan Genocide. Learn about the events leading up to and during genocide on this BBC webpage (text and video clips): http://www.bbc.com/news/world-africa-26875506.

- What parallels can you draw between *The Enemy* and the BBC's summary of the Rwandan Genocide?

- Hand out blank Venn diagrams to table groups, and ask them to add facts from both media (the book and the BBC report) to their diagram. What points of intersection appear in the middle, where the circles overlap? What common themes are revealed? (Optional: Participants can use drawings instead of words to fill in the diagram.)

- Ask groups to think of analogous situations in the world today. What similarities can they find between a situation today and either situation in the diagram?

- Have groups share and compare their Venn diagrams. As each group is sharing, compile on the board the current examples that are shared to help others make an immediate connection to the activity.

ASSESSMENT:

- Whole-group discussion using Venn diagram data and individual participants' interpretations.

VENN DIAGRAM

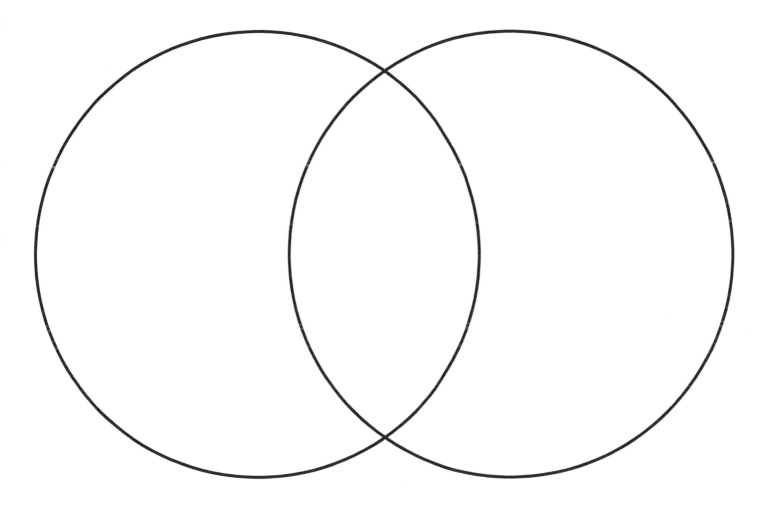

TEACHER LESSON 2: CRISIS IN SYRIA

Objectives	Extend knowledge of the refugee experience through the example of Syria
Themes	**THEME 1:** Conflict Awareness **THEME 6a:** Listening, Empathy, and Perspective-Taking
Standards and Guidelines **Competency Areas**	C2.3: Develop Productive Interactions with Clients C2.2: Communicate Effectively
Materials	• Before-and-after photos/videos from Syria, such as "War Torn Syria Before and After," YouTube video, September 8, 2016: https://www.youtube.com/watch?v=xUXaqTlc18g • The Syrian Refugee Crisis (15 short videos), IAmSyria.org: http://www.iamsyria.org/computer-lab-video-guide-lesson-on-syria.html • Pens/pencils • Paper

War has a devastating effects on civilians. The present war in Syria has resulted in a massive displacement of people and thousands of deaths. This lesson is intended to provide background on the Syrian situation as well as information on the refugee experience in general.

Note: This lesson is designed for the education of teachers. Do not do this activity with teachers who have fled from a conflict zone without speaking to them in advance. Some teachers or students will not be comfortable watching the videos and it could cause harm.

ACTIVATION:

- Share photos from Syria before and after/during the war. You can use the search phrase "Syria before and after war" to find photos and slideshows online.

- On a blank piece of paper, ask participants to write down what they currently know about the situation in Syria.
  - When/how did the crisis start?
  - What precipitated the war?
  - Who is fighting whom?
  - Who is backing whom?
  - How many civilians have been affected?
  - What has been the effect of internally displaced people? Of refugees going to other countries?

- Your group may include participants with little knowledge of the situation and participants with much prior knowledge and/or experience. Invite those with more knowledge and experience to contribute to a group discussion.

ACQUISITION:

- Have participants watch 15 short videos about the war in Syria compiled by IAmSyria.org (http://www.iamsyria.org/computer-lab-video-guide-lesson-on-syria.html). Participants can watch in a computer lab or on their own devices. Ask participants to jot down their thoughts and reactions after each video: What did they learn? What surprised them? What questions do they have? (You might choose to distribute the Video Guide available from IAmSyria.org to prompt and guide students' reflections; the guide can be downloaded from the webpage with the videos.)

APPLICATION:

- Encourage participants to reflect on the content of the various videos in a medium that works for them. Participants may be writers, singers, artists, advocates, or videographers. Have them use any medium(s) or tool(s) of their choosing. Have them consider what moved or affected them most. For example:
  - What did they see or hear that they feel strongly about?
  - Do they have a personal connection to the situation in Syria?
  - Do they know people who have emigrated to Canada as refugees from Syria?
  - What does Canada/the world need to know about the crisis in Syria?

- If any participants are willing to share their creations with the group, offer them the chance to do so.

ASSESSMENT:

- Collect the notes participants jotted down and look for evidence of understanding and connections made between the topics. In participants' personal reflections, look for comprehension of key themes in the videos: refugee movement, barrel bombs, complicated conflict, effects on children and families, difficulty with settlement.

TEACHER LESSON 3: COUNTERING STEREOTYPES – ISLAMOPHOBIA

This lesson's structure and content were informed by "Anti-Muslim Bigotry and Being an Ally," a lesson plan from the Anti-Defamation League (ADL) which contains useful vocabulary, links to news articles, examples of Islamophobic incidents, and 2 pages of myths and facts about Muslim people and Islam. The ADL lesson plan is available here:

http://www.adl.org/assets/pdf/education-outreach/anti-muslim-bigotry-and-being-an-ally.pdf.

Objectives	Comprehend experiences and incidents faced by the Muslim community Become familiar with popular myths, stereotypes, and misinformation about Islam and those who adhere to this faith Reflect on why stereotypes develop, their consequences, and how to mitigate them
Themes	**THEME 1:** Conflict Awareness **THEME 5:** Building Personal and Community Connections
***Standards and Guidelines* Competency Areas**	2.3: Develop Productive Interactions with Clients

Materials	• Videos:
	  • "10 Myths About Islam" (Geobeats, 2014): https://www.youtube.com/watch?v=SInvcvpbaQQ
	  • "Top 10 Misconceptions about Muslims" (Karim Jovian, 2015): https://www.youtube.com/watch?v=iUvnD5GVAXg&t=9s
	  • "How religious are so-called 'Islamic terrorists'?" (Al Jazeera UpFront, 2016): https://www.youtube.com/watch?v=Vop1ZNIc_j8
	• Pencils/pens
	• Paper

Since 9/11, the war on terror has been a hot topic in the media and within governments. With the emergence of ISIS/ISIL/Daesh, this discussion has intensified. Lack of information and misuse of information has led to mass generalizations and futile talks whereby the religion of Islam is conflated with terrorism. We see a rise in anti-Muslim sentiments as well as public misunderstandings.

Note: There may be Muslim participants in your group. Some of them might be comfortable discussing these issues, whilst others may feel very nervous. Provide an advanced warning of the contents of the lesson. Discuss the content privately with any known Muslim participants prior to conducting this session.

ACTIVATION:

- Start by sharing information about Islam with participants. If possible, invite a guest speaker to the session. The focus should be on faith versus culture and the diversity of Islamic faith.

- Ask participants the following questions:
    - When you hear about a terrorist attack somewhere, what thoughts come to mind? Write down a few words that describe your thoughts.
    - What do you hear from your friends, family, or the media when there is a terrorist attack somewhere?
    - Who do you think is the target of such terrorist attacks? Who are the victims?
    - Have participants share some of their responses with the larger group to reveal different perspectives across the group.

- Watch the following videos:
    - 10 Myths About Islam: https://www.youtube.com/watch?v=SInvcvpbaQQ
    - Top 10 Misconceptions about Muslims: https://www.youtube.com/watch?v=iUvnD5GVAXg&t=9s
    - UpFront - How religious are so-called 'Islamic terrorists'? (Mehdi Hasan) https://www.youtube.com/watch?v=Vop1ZNIc_j8

- After briefly discussing myths about Islam and Muslims presented in the videos, introduce the topic of Islamophobia. Here are some relevant questions to ask participants:
    - What have you heard about Islamophobia? [Explain what Islamophobia means if there is a lack of clarity or consensus.]
    - Let's talk about stereotypes: Do you think there is a connection between Islamophobia and stereotypes of Muslim people?
    - Have you heard about any incidents where Muslims or people perceived to be Muslims were targeted?
    - Explain or give a brief account of different Islamophobic incidents that have taken place in recent times.

ACQUISITION:

- Having discussed some of the incidents, engage participants in a critical discussion of Islamophobia by asking:
    - What is happening? What is the context? Why are these incidents occurring?
    - How do you feel when you hear about incidents associated with Islamophobia? Have you had similar experiences?
    - Is it appropriate to relate Islamophobia to what is experienced by non-Muslim people (e.g., Indigenous people, minorities) who might be facing similar incidents?
    - What do all these incidents have in common?

- Guide/facilitate discussion on how these incidents might be prevented.

APPLICATION:

- Invite participants to express themselves on the following points:
    - Did anything discussed or viewed surprise you?
    - What have you learned in this session?
    - Where do the myths and misinformation discussed come from? What can happen when somebody blindly believes these myths?

- How do we mitigate the spread of misinformation, stereotypes, and perceptions?
- Can the information you received in this session change people's views about Islam and Muslims?
- If you see or hear about something Islamophobic, how will you react/respond?

ASSESSMENT:

- Ask participants to write down some of the things they have learned and how these can be applied in different situations. If they feel comfortable doing so, participants can volunteer to share their ideas with the large group or table group.

TEACHER LESSON 4: MYTHS ABOUT LANGUAGE ACQUISITION

Objectives	Increase knowledge of language acquisition to dispel myths about language learning
Themes	**THEME 4d:** Who is the E/FAL Student?
Standards and Guidelines Competency Areas	C2.3: Develop Productive Interactions with Clients
Materials	• "Three Myths About Language Fluency People Still Believe" (Babbel, 2015): https://www.youtube.com/watch?v=sU0zagnWeh8 • True and False signs • "Myths and Misconceptions About Second Language Learning: What Every Teacher Needs to Unlearn" by Barry McLaughlin (National Center for Research on Cultural Diversity and Second Language Learning, University of California, Santa Cruz, 1992): https://people.ucsc.edu/~mclaugh/MYTHS.htm • Chart paper • Markers • Tape

ANTICIPATORY SET:

- Watch the video "Three Myths About Language Fluency People Still Believe": https://www.youtube.com/watch?v=sU0zagnWeh8.

- Ask participants if they have any comments or thoughts about the video that they would like to share.

ACTIVATION:

- Post signs reading True and False on opposite sides of the room.

- Tell the group that you are going to read out a series of statements. After each statement, participants should move to the side of the room that matches their belief about the statement. Ask the participants gathered on each side of the room to give reasons for their choice before reading the next statement. Statements to be read out:

  - Children learn additional languages quickly and easily.
  - The younger the child, the more skillfully he/she will acquire an additional language.
  - The more time students spend in an additional-language context, the more quickly they learn the language.
  - Children have acquired an additional language once they can speak it.
  - All children learn an additional language in the same way.

ACQUISITION:

- Break the large group into five smaller groups, and assign each small group one myth from the article "Myths and Misconceptions about Second Language Learning: What Every Teacher Needs to Unlearn" by Barry McLaughlin.

- On chart paper, ask each group to provide an overview of the myth and answers to the following questions:
  - This article is quite old. Do you feel that these myths persist today? Why or why not?
  - Do you agree that "every teacher" needs to unlearn these ideas?
  - Explain how you would address this myth in your school with a colleague, resource teacher, or administrator who might feel that this myth is true.

- Allow small groups time to reflect on the myth and the above questions before they present their myth and additional information back to the large group.

- Allow members from other small groups to contribute their thoughts and ideas at the end of the presentation of each myth.

- After all groups have reported to the large group, invite participants to share other myths they have heard.

APPLICATION:

- Given the preceding activities and discussion, ask participants how they would respond to the following situation: A student comes to speak to you after class. They communicate very well orally, face-to-face, and they want to be moved out of E/FAL instruction to join the regular classroom full time.

ASSESSMENT:

- Ask participants to write down some new learnings from the session and how these can be used in the classroom setting. If they feel comfortable doing so, participants can share their ideas with the large group or table group.

TEACHER LESSON 5: OPTIONS FOR POST-SECONDARY EDUCATION

Objectives	Explore education and training institutions in the community that meet student needs and interests
Themes	**THEME 2:** Social Determinants of Health **THEME 5:** Building Personal and Community Connections
Standards and Guidelines Competency Areas	C3.1: Possess Career Development Knowledge C4.1: Refer Clients to the Appropriate Sources
Materials	• Pens/pencils • Completed mind maps from Teacher Lesson 29: Multiple Intelligences (p. 140-141) or list/map of career options in different fields (see below) • Computers/laptops/tablets/smartphones and Wi-Fi (for research) • Chart paper or poster paper

Conversations around life and career goals and planning can occur at any time. Having a basic understanding of how to pursue these goals and what kinds of institutions are in your community is not solely the responsibility of guidance and career counsellors. It can be an important asset in opening dialogue, inspiring curiosity, and meeting student needs.

There are many opportunities for post-secondary training and education that suit a variety of goals and interests. These range from a certificate program that can be completed in under a year to several years of formal university academics. Examining requirements for options within a field can reveal the right fit (interest, budget, timeframe). Participants will need a list or map of career options in different fields to complete this lesson. Creating such maps is the goal of Lesson 29, Multiple Intelligences; complete that lesson with participants before you do this one, or else obtain a list/map of career options from another source beforehand.

ACTIVATION:

- Poll participants to gauge familiarity with available education and training institutions:
  - What institutions are in your area?
  - What programs do they offer?
  - What do you know about the application process?
  - What are the requirements (high school diploma, mature student, etc.)?
  - Discuss goals and plans teachers have heard from students regarding their futures.
  - What kind of careers are students interested in?
  - What barriers to post-secondary education do they face?
  - What myths or misunderstandings regarding post-secondary education do you know/hear?

ACQUISITION:

- Extract career options that were identified in the mind maps from Multiple Intelligences (Teacher Lesson 29, p. 138) or from other sources, and divide them among individuals in the group.

- Investigate the following for each career choice:
  - Where can you find appropriate education/training?
  - What are the entrance requirements?
  - How much will it cost?
  - How long will it take?
  - What kind of accreditation will you receive (certificate, diploma, degree, etc.)?
  - What are the salary expectations upon entry into the field?
  - Are there jobs available in the country? Your province/territory? Your region? Your area?
  - Does the institution help with employment placements?

- Organize information using one piece of chart or poster paper for each field/industry, to create a visual representation of potential career options and pathways to employment. Create a point-form list to accompany the representation that identifies
  - challenges in locating information,
  - challenges for students in attending identified programs, and
  - supports for students in attending identified programs.

APPLICATION:

- Take turns presenting findings to the large group.

- Prompt discussion with these questions:
  - What did you learn?
  - Did anything surprise you?
  - Do you feel better equipped to engage in conversations with students about their interests and goals?
  - What additional information do you need?
  - What strategies can you use to help students actively locate information for themselves?
  - How can we make information better available to students?

ASSESSMENT:

- Ask participants to write down some of the things they have learned and how these can be applied in different situations. If they feel comfortable doing so, participants can share their ideas with the large group or table group.

TEACHER LESSON 6: LOCAL RESOURCES AND SUPPORTS

Objectives	Identify local resources and supports for students/families experiencing issues related to the social determinants of health
Themes	**THEME 2:** Social Determinants of Health **THEME 5:** Building Personal and Community Connections
Standards and Guidelines **Competency Areas**	C2.1: Respect Diversity C4.1: Refer Clients to the Appropriate Sources
Materials	• Chart paper and/or poster board • Sticky notes or markers/pens in 6 different colours • Various materials, as required, to create a PSA (e.g., video camera, paper)

ANTICIPATORY SET:

Discuss the various roles educators undertake beyond teaching subject-area curriculum and the resources available to help them fulfill those roles. Knowing about the supports available within a school division and in the greater community can help educators ensure all student (and family) needs are met. Developing relationships and partnerships with these service providers creates opportunities for open and ongoing dialogue.

ACTIVATION:

- As a large group, identify issues related to the social determinants of health that students and their families commonly experience in your school/area (e.g., homelessness, unemployment, hunger). Write each of these issues on the board or on chart paper, leaving ample space to add information that arises from discussions.

- Break up into table groups or pairs. Assign (or have small groups choose) issues identified by the large group until they are all distributed. On poster board or chart paper (one per issue), pairs/groups use 3 different colours to record
  - the issue,
  - signs of the issue in the classroom (How would you know this may be something going on with your student?), and
  - risks (What might happen if the issue continues without support or resources?).

  Participants may record their responses in any format (e.g., columns, table, web).

- Return to the large-group list and open a discussion around learning expectations for students who are experiencing any of the difficult issues listed.
  - Why is it important for teachers to identify the issue and respond?
  - What happens if teachers don't address the issue?
  - What is the harm in assuming someone else will take care of it?

ACQUISITION:

- Have small groups/pairs return to their poster board. (Time for research may be required for this part or the research can be assigned as "homework".) Again using a different colour for each category, groups identify resources to address their situations/issues available within
  - their school,
  - their school division, and
  - the community.

- Bring the large group together to discuss and share resources and strategies teachers can use to reduce the stress and burden of assuming multiple roles in the classroom. List the resources and strategies on chart paper at the front of the room. Identify areas where supports are lacking.

APPLICATION/ASSESSMENT:

- Using their poster boards as a reference, each group/pair creates a public service announcement (PSA) for one of their issues. If more than one group is working on the same issue, identify a different audience for each PSA (e.g., one group targets students, another parents/caregivers, another school staff).

- The PSA can be in any form (e.g., poster, brochure, video, radio ad). It should help lead the audience to helpful resources. It should be easily understood by people with different language levels.

TEACHER LESSON 7: RESTORATIVE PRACTICES IN THE CLASSROOM

Objectives	Learn how and why to address negative behaviours with restorative practices
Themes	**THEME 3a:** Restorative Practices and Justice
Standards and Guidelines **Competency Areas**	C2.2: Communicate Effectively
Materials	• Paper • Pens/pencils

Restorative practices in the classroom not only build and maintain community, but can produce teachable moments, generate understanding of self and values, and strengthen relationships.

One of the most important things for educators to remember is that conflicts and offensive and inappropriate behaviour will occur; the goal is to guide students to restore relationships and/or property—to understand what went wrong and how their behaviour affects others, and to make amends based on intrinsic motivation.

ACTIVATION:

- In table groups of 3 or 4, share some of the behaviour concerns you see in your classroom or school and how they are dealt with. Discuss possible causes (e.g., boredom, irritation, frustration, unaware of social/cultural expectations).

- Share discussed behaviours with the whole group, tracking them on the board. Add comments or thoughts from other groups after each table group has had an opportunity to share.

ACQUISITION:

Suspensions, detentions, removal from class, being withheld from special events or field trips, and having other privileges revoked are well-known strategies for behaviour management.

- Create a diagram or chart to discuss the differences between restorative and punitive practices. Include the desired goal and how it might be achieved with each method. A sample diagram has been started here:

Restorative Methods	Goal	Punative Methods
• developing resonsibility • accountability • strengthen relationship	• establish self-motivated positive behaviour and values	• shaming • guilt • power-based

- Discuss:
  - Do punitive methods achieve the goal? Why or why not?
  - Do restorative methods achieve the goal? Why or why not?
  - What happens to the relationship between "offender" and others with each of these methods?

APPLICATION:

- Return to the behaviours identified by the original table groups. Create a table to list punitive and restorative approaches—and their potential outcomes—for four different behaviours/situations (names may be changed to maintain confidentiality). Example:

Description of Behaviour/Incident	Punitive Approach	Potential Outcomes	Restorative Approach	Potential Outcomes
Sahra is playing outside at recess. She becomes quite warm and removes her hijab. Her brother sees and becomes angry, striking her as he yells for her to put it back on. *Hitting is socially/ culturally unacceptable behaviour.*	Reprimand Detention Call parents	Possibility of changed behaviour if/ once cultural difference is understood. Unknown status of child-teacher relationship. Potential for embarrassment, anger, frustration.	Opportunity to explain importance of hijab Discussion of alternative responses to sister Discussion about socially/culturally acceptable responses Reasoned apology	Cross-cultural learning Reinforced child-teacher relationship Maintained sibling relationship Behaviour change based on learning/ understanding

ASSESSMENT:

- Write a personal reflection identifying your current practice.
  - Do you already take a restorative approach? How?
  - What changes and/or improvements would you like to make to your practice?

TEACHER LESSON 8: PRIVILEGE WALK

Objectives	Identify strategies to enhance inclusivity and fairness in the classroom
Themes	**THEME 3b:** Equity **THEME 6a:** Listening, Empathy, and Perspective-Taking
Standards and Guidelines **Competency Areas**	C2.2: Communicate Effectively C3.1: Possess Career Development Knowledge
Materials	• Projector • Pencils/pens and paper • Scrap paper and a bucket or recycling bin • "Equity, Equality, and Inclusion" (DirectCourse, 2017): http://directcourseonline.com/equity-equality-inclusion/ • "The Problem with that Equity vs. Equality Graph You're Using" by Paul Kuttner (CulturalOrganizing.org, 2016): http://culturalorganizing.org/the-problem-with-that-equity-vs-equality-graphic/ • Privilege Walk: Instructions (p. 69) • Privilege Walk: Situations and Events (p. 70-71) • Privilege Walk: Role Cards (pp. 72-75) on card stock or regular paper and cut

ANTICIPATORY SET:
• Project the image found here:
http://directcourseonline.com/wp-content/uploads/2017/02/Equity-Equality-Graphic.jpg

• Ask participants to write down their initial responses to these questions:
  • What do you see with your eyes?
  • What do you feel with your heart?
  • What are you wondering with your head?

ACTIVATION:
The following is a simplified version of a simulation originally posted to BuzzFeed.com (https://www.buzzfeed.com/nathanwpyle/this-teacher-taught-his-class-a-powerful-lesson-about-privil?utm_term=.iozZQA7XA#.evkZ58ly8)
• Place participants in 5 rows of chairs.
• Give each person a sheet of scrap paper to crumple into a ball.
• Put a bucket or recycling bin at the front of the room, a few steps away from the first row.
• Ask each person to throw their ball into the bucket.

ACQUISITION:

- Debrief:
    - How did it feel trying to throw the paper into the bucket?
    - How did it feel to sit in the front row? How did it feel to sit in the back?
    - What was the message of the simulation?
    - What can you do as a person sitting in the front and knowing people are behind you?

- Break the large group into smaller groups and give one of the following articles to each group. (Before leading this session, please check the internet for more-current articles so that the conversation is connected to current knowledge.)
    - "Equity, Equality, and Inclusion": http://directcourseonline.com/equity-equality-inclusion/
    - "The Problem with that Equity vs. Equality Graph You're Using": http://culturalorganizing.org/the-problem-with-that-equity-vs-equality-graphic/

- While reading, invite participates to annotate what surprises them, what questions they have, and what next steps they could take. Allow time for debriefing.

APPLICATION:

Part 1:

- Return to the image projected at the beginning. Ask participants to revisit the questions posed at the beginning of the session (What do you see…, What do you feel…, What are you wondering…). How do they respond now, after the simulation and discussion?

- Discuss different ways and reasons to run this simulation in the classroom. Remember to consider grade level and intent. Ask: Would this be a "nice to do" or a "need to do" in your classroom?

Part 2:

- Distribute a Role Card to each participant. Remind them to keep their card private.

- Read the instructions for the Privilege Walk aloud, and then use the situations and events to engage in the activity.

ASSESSMENT:

- Debrief the activity by asking questions such as these:
    - What happened in this activity?
    - How easy or difficult was it to play your role?
    - What did you imagine the person you were playing was like? How did you feel, imagining yourself as that person? Is that person like you in any way? Do you know anyone like that person?

- Relate the activity to issues of immigration, discrimination, and social and economic inequality by asking questions such as these:
    - How did people feel stepping forward—or not?
    - If you stepped forward often, when did you begin to notice that others were not moving as fast as you were?
    - Did the person you were imagining yourself to be move ahead or not? Why?
    - Did you feel that something was unfair?
    - Is what happened in this activity anything like what happens in the real world? How?
    - What gives some people in our community more opportunities than others? Fewer opportunities?

PRIVILEGE WALK:
INSTRUCTIONS TO PARTICIPANTS

Read the following aloud to participants:

1. Imagine that you are someone else, someone who may be quite different from yourself.

2. Everyone takes a Role Card. This card is your new identity. Read silently and do not let anyone know who you are. If you do not understand anything about your role, silently raise your hand and wait for me to come and explain.

3. Silently line up beside each other, as if on a starting line.

4. I am going to describe some things that might happen to a person. If the statement would be true for the person you are imagining yourself to be, then you should take a step forward. Otherwise you should not move. Remember to just imagine what you think the answer is based on the limited information that you have. You do not have to worry about whether you are right or wrong because it is you that is imagining what it is like to be that person.

5. I am going to read out the situations one at a time. I will pause between each statement to allow you time to step forward. You are allowed to look around to see where others are. But you are not allowed to chat, groan, cheer, or make any other sound. You are representing real people so making sounds could be hurtful to someone else in the room with similar realities. This is a silent activity.

6. At the end of the activity, everyone can sit down in their final position. Everyone will be able to describe who they were. Take time to observe where you are at the end of the activity.

PRIVILEGE WALK:
SITUATIONS AND EVENTS

Read the following situations aloud. After reading out each situation, give the participants time to determine what their 'role' would do. Ask them to step forward if they believe the statement is true for their role. Ask them to look where they are relative to others. Alter the situations and events as needed to fit the audience and intent.

1. You and your family always have enough money to meet your needs.

2. You and your family always have enough money to meet the wants of everyone in your house.

3. You live in a decent place with a telephone / cell phone and television.

4. You are not teased or excluded because of your different appearance or disability.

5. The people you live with ask your opinion about major decisions that concern you.

6. You go to a good school and participate in after-school clubs and sports.

7. You take extra lessons after school in music and drawing.

8. You are not afraid of being stopped by the police.

9. You live with adults who love you and always have your best interests at heart.

10. You have never felt discriminated against because of your or your parents' origins, background, religion, or culture.

11. You have regular medical and dental check-ups, even when you are not sick.

12. You and your family go away on holiday once a year.

13. You can invite friends for dinner or to sleep over at your home.

14. When you are older, you can go to university or choose any job or profession you like.

15. You are not afraid of being teased or attacked in the streets, at school, or where you live.

16. You usually see people on TV or in films who look and live as you do.

17. You and your family go to the movies, the zoo, a museum, the countryside, or other fun places at least once a month.

18. Your parents and grandparents and even great-grandparents were all born in this country.

19. You get new clothes and shoes whenever you need them.

20. You have plenty of time to play and friends to play with.

21. You have access to a computer and can use the internet.

22. You feel appreciated for what you can do and encouraged to develop all your abilities.

23. You think you are going to have a happy future when you grow up.

PRIVILEGE WALK: ROLE CARDS

Alter the Role Cards as needed to fit the audience and intent.

✂ -

You are 8 years old. You and your two brothers live in a nice house with a big garden and a swimming pool. Your father is the manager of a bank in your town. Your mother takes care of the house and family. Everyone in your family was born in the same city.

You are 20 years old. You were born in this town, but your parents moved here from Asia. They run a nice restaurant, and you live in rooms above the restaurant with your sister. After university classes, you and your sister help run the restaurant because that is expected in your family.

You are 15 years old. You live in a farmhouse in the country. Your father is a farmer and your mother takes care of the family finances. You have three brothers and one sister. You must feed the animals before the school bus arrives. The town is about 45 minutes from your home. After school you have to practice your piano for 60 minutes.

You are 10 years old. You are an only child. You live alone with your mother in an apartment in the city. Your mother works in a factory, 8 hours a day. You are very good at music and dancing, but your mother can not afford to pay for both activities so you have to pick one. To help pay the bills, you clean homes in the apartment building.

You are 12 years old. You recently arrived from Syria. You grew up at the edge of a small village, in a small house with no bathroom. You have six brothers and sisters. You speak excellent English but your parents are just learning.

You are 13 years old. You were born with a disability and have to use a wheelchair. You live in an apartment in the city with your parents and two sisters. Your dad is a nurse and your mom is a teacher. Family summer vacations are difficult but your favourite time of year.

You are 11 years old. You have lived in 12 different foster homes since the age of 3. You don't know who your parents are or where they are. You do not enjoy school. You prefer to sit by yourself and draw. That is the only way you can get away from all of the strangers that are raising you.

You are 9 years old and have an identical twin. You live in social housing where the government pays most of the rent for your family. Your mother takes you to school every day. She works in a department store in the evenings, so you stay at the community centre in the evening. Your father is in jail.

You are 14 years old and an only child. You live in a small house in a town with your parents. Your father is a construction worker and your mother delivers mail. You are very good at sports.

You are 11 years old. You and your parents came to this country to find safety from the war going on in your home country, Somalia. You have been here for three years. You don't know when you can go home again. Your parents are learning English during the day. You have a baby sister.

You are 13, the oldest of six children. Your father drives a truck and is away a lot, and your mother is a waitress who often has to work at night. You have to babysit a lot. You are in charge of getting your siblings to school before you go to your school. You have to leave school early in order to pick everyone up.

You are 17 years old. Your parents divorced when you were a baby. You live with your mother and her boyfriend. On weekends, you visit your father and his new wife and their two small children in a nearby city. Your parents are both employed so you are allowed to play soccer, your favourite sport.

You are 11 years old. You have lived with different foster parents since you were a small child because your parents couldn't take care of you. Your foster parents are nice. Four other foster children also live in the same small house as you.

You are 8 years old. You and your sister live with your grandparents in a small town out in the country. Your parents are divorced and your mother works as a secretary in the city. You rarely see your father.

You are 10 years old and the tallest in your class. You have a learning disability that makes you two classes behind in school. Both your parents work a lot so they don't have much time to help you with homework.

You are 6 years old. Your mother died when you were born. Your father remarried and you live with him, your stepmother, and her two daughters. The two daughter are teenagers. Your father is a lawyer. You have a huge house. There are a lot of people always around.

You are 8 years old and the youngest of three children. Your family lives in a small apartment in a big city. Your father is a mechanic but he is out of work right now, so you don't have much money. But your father has more time to play with you. Your mom is not in your life.

You are 10 years old. You immigrated to this country when you were a baby. Many other immigrants live in your neighborhood, where your father has a shop. You speak the languages of both your new and old countries and often translate for your mother and grandmother.

You are 11 years old. You live in a village in the country with your parents and a younger brother and sister. Your parents run a bakery. They are very busy baking from 4 a.m. until 6 p.m. You are sometimes teased because you are overweight. You are in charge of getting yourself and siblings to school every morning by bus. When you finally get home after school you have about 60 minutes of free time before everyone has to go to sleep.

You are 13. You have asthma and have to miss a lot of school because you are sick, especially in winter. You spend a lot of time at home in bed watching TV, surfing the internet, and playing video games. It's lonely because both your parents go out to work.

You are 11. You are the child of the Canadian ambassador in your country. You go to the international school. You wear thick glasses and stammer a little. Your family has moved a lot and your parents are very busy, especially in the evenings.

You are 8 years old. You and your older brother are very talented at mathematics, physics, languages and, in fact, most things. Your parents are university professors. They send you to special courses and training camps all the time to prepare for competitions.

You are 11. While your school friends are eating lunch at school you cannot because you are Muslim. During Ramadan, you have to fast from dawn to sunset. Your friends tease you because of this. You don't have very many Muslim friends at school, but after school your family drives across the city to hang out with all your cousins. Your mom stays at home and your dad is a scientist at the local college.

You are 8. Most of your friends celebrate Christmas. You do not; you are Jewish so you celebrate Chanukah. Your friends get a Christmas tree but you get to light candles for 8 days in a row. Some people think that is weird, but not your friends. Your two parents run a restaurant together. You have no siblings.

You are 13 years old. Your family works hard to pay all the bills on time. You and your three sisters all play hockey so your mom works an extra job to pay for ice time and equipment. Last weekend, as your team entered the ice rink, fans in the stands called you a squaw and made fun of your two long dark-haired braids.

You are 10 years old. Your mom is Jewish and your dad is Catholic. Most of the time it is easy to celebrate both religions. However, your Catholic grandparents do not like your Jewish grandparents, so some holidays are difficult. Right now, the family is deciding what school you should go to—a private Catholic school or a private Jewish school. Both schools are not near your home, so you have no friends at either school.

You are 12 years old. You do not have a mom, so you live with your dad. He has a hard time getting up in the morning, so your school feeds you. You once had a friend over but they laughed at the dream catcher in your room so you won't do that again.

You are 10 years old. You have two moms. One mom was born in the Philippines. The other mom is new to our city. One mom works full-time while the other mom stays home on disability insurance due to a workplace accident.

You are 12 years old. You and your parents live in a small house in the inner city. Your father works at home writing novels. Your mother travels a lot for her job. Your parents do not allow you to watch television or play with friends that they do not know. They want you to become a doctor, even though you are afraid of blood.

You are 16 years old. You were born in Mexico to parents who are migrant workers. Every year for 5 months you have to move to southern Ontario so that everyone can work in the tomato fields and factories. This year while in Canada, you decide to stay for school with another family. They are very kind and allow you to play sports but you miss your family especially over the holidays.

TEACHER LESSON 9: SCAFFOLDING ACADEMIC LEARNING FOR ADDITIONAL LANGUAGE LEARNERS

Objectives	Extend knowledge of scaffolding for students learning additional languages
Themes	**THEME 4:** Refugee Characteristics **THEME 4d:** Who is the E/FAL Student? **THEME 3b:** Equity
Standards and Guidelines **Competency Areas**	C2.1: Respect Diversity C3.1: Possess Career Development Knowledge
Materials	• "Scaffolding Academic Learning for Second Language Learners," by Karen Sue Bradley and Jack Alden Bradley (The Internet TESL Journal, Vol. X, No. 5, May 2004): http://iteslj.org/Articles/Bradley-Scaffolding/ • Sample texts that could be used with participants' students

ANTICIPATORY SET:

Scaffolding refers to providing contextual supports for meaning through the use of simplified language, teacher modelling, visuals and graphics, cooperative learning, and hands-on learning (Ovando, Collier, & Combs, 2003, p. 345)

- Remind participants that as proficiency grows, scaffolding can be reduced or removed.

- Introduce participants to the three types of scaffolding they will read about during the lesson:
  - Simplifying the language: The teacher can simplify the language by shortening selections, speaking in the present tense, and avoiding the use of idioms.
  - Asking for completion, not generation: The teacher can have students choose answers from a list or complete a partially finished outline or paragraph.
  - Using visuals: The teacher can present information and ask for students to respond through the use of graphic organizers, tables, charts, outlines, and graphs.

ACTIVATION:
- Discussion questions:
  - To what extent should the teacher scaffold the English language learning of students?
  - What if students' conversational skills vary greatly from their written skills?
  - What are the criteria for ending scaffolding? Who decides that?

ACQUISITION:
- Have participants read the article "Scaffolding Academic Learning for Second Language Learners." Review and discuss the article as a group, and revisit the activation questions.

APPLICATION:

- Provide sample texts that contain challenging words for E/FAL students and ask participants to work in groups to create scaffolding ideas for the texts. Return to the larger group to share ideas.

ASSESSMENT:

- Ask participants to write down some of issues related to scaffolding that come to mind in relation to refugee and newcomer students learning English or French as an additional language. If they feel comfortable doing so, participants can share their ideas with the large group or table group.

2

TEACHER LESSON 10: REFUGEE NARRATIVES AND CASE STUDIES

Objectives	Learn more about refugees' experiences to develop greater empathy and respect for the life experiences of refugee students
Themes	**THEME 4:** Refugee Characteristics **THEME 5:** Building Personal and Community Connections
Standards and Guidelines **Competency Areas**	C2.1: Respect Diversity C3.1: Refer Clients to the Appropriate Sources
Materials	• Supporting Refugee Children: Strategies for Educators by Jan Stewart (Toronto, ON: University of Toronto Press, 2011) • Building Hope: Refugee Learner Narratives (Manitoba Education and Training, 2015; 11 narratives in total) http://www.edu.gov.mb.ca/k12/docs/support/building_hope/index.html • (optional) Letters to Our Children: The Memories, Challenges & Dreams of Mothers New to Canada (KidBridge Press, 2014), available online at http://www.mcnallyrobinson.com/9780991886210/various/letters-to-our-children • Large map of the world OR printed maps of the world for each table group • Chart paper • Pens and/or markers • Sticky notes

Note: This lesson involves a significant amount of reading for participants and is suitable for a half-day workshop.

ANTICIPATORY SET:
  • Post the following for participants to read:

According to the United Nations High Commissioner for Refugees (UNHCR), by the end of 2016, 65.6 million individuals around the world were displaced as a result of persecution, conflict, violence, or human rights violations.

  • 22.5 million refugees
  • 40.3 million internally displaced people
  • 2.8 million asylum-seekers
            (UNHCR, 2017b, p. 2)

- Ask participants to reflect on these statistics and to comment on what this means for them as classroom teachers. What do they know now, and what do they think they need to learn?

ACTIVATION:

- Read Sokut's story from the prologue of Jan Stewart's *Supporting Refugee Children: Strategies for Educators*. Afterward, ask each participant to share one word that summarizes the story or describes how it made them feel.

- Remind the group of the danger of focusing on a single story. There are *many* different stories of immigrants' and refugees' experiences. The narratives participants will encounter in this session are just a small sample of peoples' lived experiences. It is important to be open and non-judgmental toward students and their experiences.

ACQUISITION:

- Assign one narrative from *Building Hope: Refugee Learner Narratives* to each table group. Each narrative tells of one refugee's journey and experiences in coming to Canada.
    - Anam (Burundi)
    - Angelica (Democratic Republic of the Congo)
    - Bandiri (Somalia)
    - Favor (Democratic Republic of the Congo)
    - Keza (Rwanda)
    - Layla (Somalia)
    - Mary (South Sudan)
    - Mustapha (Sierra Leone)
    - Nevaeh (Sierra Leone)
    - Tanya (Afghanistan)
    - Yodu (South Sudan)

Note: Additional narratives from other regions can be found in Letters to Our Children: The Memories, Challenges & Dreams of Mothers New to Canada (KidBridge Press, 2014), available from http://www.mcnallyrobinson.com/9780991886210/various/letters-to-our-children.

- Have each table group answer the following questions about their refugee:
    1. What were some of your refugee's migration and pre-migration experiences?
    2. What would you say was successful in terms of this person's settlement in Canada?
    3. What challenges did this person face settling in Canada (post-migration)?
    4. What did you see in this person's story that could be considered a best practice/strategy?
    5. Make a list of some local/community resources that you could connect refugee students to, to help support them.

- Table groups can use chart paper, a map, and pens/markers to draw or document the path of their refugee and highlights in their story.

- Have each table group present their refugee's story to the group, including a summary of their answers to the above questions.

APPLICATION:

- After hearing the cases, have table groups answer the following questions:
  - What common themes do you see through all the narratives?
  - What are some of the effects of war? Resettlement?
  - What helped these students? What hindered these students?
  - What have you learned about refugee students after hearing and discussing these cases? What should all teachers know about refugee students?
  - How can teachers support refugee students in schools?

ASSESSMENT:

- Write each of the following questions at the top of a different sheet of chart paper. Post the sheets around the room. Participants write their answers and comments on sticky notes and add them the appropriate sheets.
  - What surprised you?
  - What moved you?
  - What did you learn from hearing the stories?
  - How will you change what you do in teaching refugee students as a result?
  - How will you increase inclusivity for refugee students in regular classroom activities?

TEACHER LESSON 11: REFUGEE CASE STUDIES

Objectives	Connect common classroom-based issues faced by refugee and newcomer students with potential solutions
Themes	**THEME4:** Refugee Characteristics **THEME 4d:** Who is the E/FAL Student? **THEME 6:** Cultural Competency / Culturally Responsive Teaching
Standards and Guidelines Competency Areas	C2.2: Communicate Effectively C2.1: Respect Diversity C2.3: Develop Positive Interactions with Clients
Materials	• 20 Case Studies (pp. 83-88) cut into strips • Paper • Pens/pencils

ANTICIPATORY SET:

- Ask participants to reflect on media reports about issues facing refugees. Do any of these issues affect students in the school system?

ACTIVATION:

- Ask participants to share some challenges and successes that refugee and newcomer students might experience in the school system. Compile a list on the board as participants call out responses.

- Ask: Based on the challenges and successes you have experienced in your work with refugee and newcomer students, what worked? What didn't work? What made things easier? What complicated things? As participants respond, try to connect their ideas to the challenges and successes already listed.

Note: If the group lacks sufficient experience to develop a list, brainstorm what participants believe would be the greatest challenges and potential solutions. If no list emerges, lead a general discussion to enhance basic knowledge of common concerns.

ACQUISITION:

- Divide participants into groups of 2–3 and assign each group one case study from the collection on pages 81-86.
  - The case studies are from different points of view (administrator, teacher, support staff).
  - Participants may need to make one or more assumptions about each case, depending on the circumstances and detail.

- Ask participants to imagine that this is their role/job and to do their best to find a solution. Invite them to consider the following:
  - What will they do?
  - Who will they involve?
  - What steps will they take?
  - Who can help them?

APPLICATION:

- Say: You have spent time learning and thinking about issues that affect children from refugee backgrounds. Using what you have learned and what you have heard from others today, compile your own case study for us to work on. Use a personal experience, one you have heard from another person, or a scenario that you worry about or anticipate encountering in the future.
  - Ask: From whose perspective will you write your case study?
  - Tell participants to be realistic, and to ensure the case study adequately covers the complexity of what an educator might potentially encounter in a school, the community, the school division, or the department.

ASSESSMENT:

- Collect the case studies. Look for common themes, systemic collaboration, and realistic and holistic solutions.

CASE STUDIES
(Written by Jan Stewart, 2017)

1. Career Road Block

Sahab is a new student in grade 10. He has three siblings—two brothers (grade 7 and grade 4) and a baby sister. Sahab has disclosed to his teacher that there is hardly any food at home. His mother and father work two jobs each. Both parents are well educated, but neither of them can get work in Canada in the fields for which they have been trained. Sahab's mom was a licensed pharmacist and Sahab's dad was a carpenter back in Colombia. You are Sahab's teacher and you notice that he seems sad, so you talk to him privately. Sahab wants to go to university and become an engineer and so far, he is doing very well in all his courses. He tells you that because of his family situation, his parents need him to quit school to get a job so he can provide for the family; this is what is causing his sadness. Sahab does not want to quit school and desperately wants to graduate and go to university. He cannot talk to his parents about his career plans and feels like there is no way out for him. He will need to quit school and start working at the end of the current term.

How can you help Sahab?

2. A Litany of Complaints

Three teachers have come to talk to you, the school principal of a high school with a population of about 600 students. The three teachers are your leading teachers. They are very strong and rarely complain about anything. In their meeting with you, they bring up several issues that they think are negatively affecting the learning of refugee and newcomer students at your school. One of the teachers has personally witnessed teachers being harsh and rude to the African students, and in the staff room last week, this teacher said, "Those Africans do not belong in our schools and they are taking away from quality teaching time in my class." The teacher indicated that he thinks this particular teacher is racist and unaccepting of immigrant students. The second complaint, from a teacher/guidance counsellor, is that more and more kids are coming to him to talk about issues arising from war and conflict during their pre-migration years. At least five students have come to guidance in the last two weeks to talk about having flashbacks and stomach aches because of trauma. The third teacher tells you that she cannot sleep at night because she is worrying about several students who have discussed their experiences living through war. Many students have lost their parents and some of them saw their parents get shot or slashed by machetes. This teacher says that this is seriously affecting her mental health and she worries every day about how she can help these kids.

You are the principal, and these teachers are counting on your leadership and support. What are you going to do?

3. Counsellor's Dilemma

A student from Bhutan comes to talk about her traumatic experiences of war, torture, and sexual assault before her journey to Canada. She is unable to sleep and complains of health problems. When you suggest that there are people she can talk to who will be able help her, she refuses saying she trusts only you and is not interested in speaking to anyone else. The student also tells you that her mother will disown her if she ever finds out the girl has talked to anyone about her past. You sense that she is experiencing symptoms of trauma and you are very worried about the possibility of her harming herself.

How can you support this female student?

4. The Quiet Student

Angesia comes from the Democratic Republic of Congo. She was placed in grade 4 and since arriving into your classroom, Angesia has not said a word. She looks tired, scared, and lonely and she will not look at you when you are talking to her. You notice that when other adults enter the room, Angesia tenses up and you can see her trembling from across the room. On one particular occasion, when you are studying different careers, you bring another student's father in to talk about his job as a police officer. With one look at him, Angesia bursts into tears and runs out of the room. You call the office, but Angesia has already been intercepted by a hallway monitor who scolds her for running in the hallway. She is being reluctantly escorted to the office and the monitor is scolding her harshly telling her she has broken the school rules and will need to see the principal. You suspect that Angesia has experienced violence, but you are not sure. You sense that she is starting to trust you, but you know that this experience will set her back and make it even more difficult for you going forward.

What are your next steps as Angesia's teacher? How do you talk to the other professionals in the school without undermining their authority? What can you do to keep gaining Angesia's trust?

5. Get to Work

Anon is a grade 10 student from Sudan who is expected to work while he continues his studies. The government gave him a year to get settled and then told him that he needed a job to support himself. Anon lives with an uncle and his uncle is also expecting him to help out at home and provide for himself. You work with Anon for several weeks and help him line up a job at a local grocery store. His job is to re-stock shelves and clean at night. Anon is excited to have a job and things seem to go well for the first month. After you check his grades, however, you see that his grades in all subjects have dropped at least 10% and he is always falling asleep in class. He stopped playing soccer and rarely spends time with his former peer group. Anon works an evening shift, as this is the only shift available, and instead of finishing at midnight, he has been working until 3 am.

Anon has to work, but this is seriously affecting his school success. How do you help?

6. You're Busted

Lanya and her sister Prina are from Somalia and have been at your school for the last year. Lately, you hear other students talking about the two sisters and their trouble with gang members and criminal activity. Both girls have changed their clothes, dyed their hair, and dramatically changed their appearance. Grades have slipped for both and lately they have been coming to school late, smelling of either drugs or alcohol. You see both girls engaging in risky behaviour and even when they are at school, they are often not going to class. You have known both girls since they arrived and you are really concerned about their behaviour. When talking to another student, who was a former friend of both sisters, you learn that Lanya has an abusive boyfriend who has hurt her so seriously that she has gone to the emergency room twice. Prina and Lanya have been breaking into homes and stealing money to live on. The girls used to live at home, but since the changes, their mother has refused to let them come home until they start following her traditional values. When you talk to their mother, you learn that she is irate and fed up with them acting like street girls. She has no idea how to get them back on track. You see their trajectory spiralling downward quickly.

What can you do?

7. Kai's Pictures

Kai is in grade 2. Her family came to Canada from Sudan and she has been in your class for about three months. Lately, Kai's drawings have been violent and frightening. Last week, she drew a picture of a decapitated head with blood spurting across the room. The week before, she drew red flames coming out of village buildings with bodies lying on the ground. Today, she drew a picture of a man on top of a woman with the words, "help help!" coming from the woman's mouth. The first two pictures concerned you, but now you are putting the pieces together and are really worried about what she is trying to tell you. You ask Kai's mother to come in to talk to you. You explain your concerns and she tells you that this is just Kai's imagination and you need to ignore the child. She apologizes for her daughter's behaviour and promptly leaves.

What are you going to do?

8. One Too Many

You have been given five new students in the last three months, all of whom have refugee backgrounds. You already have 10 students, out of a total of 25, who are reading far below grade level. The last five are from the same country and lately there has been some fighting in the class and hallways because the students are from two different groups who are at war in their home country. You just got word that in two days, you will be getting three more students who are also from refugee backgrounds. Two of these new students have experienced significant violence and sometimes act out their anger in class. You are struggling to meet the needs of your class as it is, and are apprehensive about receiving more students with more problems. You tell your administrator that you don't know how you will handle all of this and she shrugs her shoulders and tells you to buck up, this is the way it is. Other teachers are in the same position and they find a way to cope.

You aren't sure what to do and are feeling all alone. What can you do?

9. Competing Priorities

An Eritrean member of the community would like to start an after-school homework club at your school. As a former refugee, he wants to give back to his community by helping students with homework and providing support to families. You are the administrator of the school and you think this is a great idea that will help many of your refugee students. You have a large newcomer/refugee population and this is just what you think your students need. You bring the idea to your parent council and they are flat out opposed to it. Instead they want you to start an enrichment club for students who need a challenge. You agree that this is also needed, but you have been trying for many years to get the community to come into the school and here you finally have someone willing to run an entire program that meets the needs of newcomers. Other programs like an enrichment club are important, but you know that an after-school program for refugee students would get these kids connected to the school and help them feel like they belong.

What can you do?

10. Burning Out

Nancy is a devoted teacher in her fifth year of teaching. Students love her and she is well respected, smart, and an excellent teacher. She is in her classroom every lunch hour, before and after school starts, and lately she has been teaching newcomer students how to cook Canadian food. Nancy's room is a safe place for newcomer students, and you know that Nancy is going above and beyond her role as a teacher to help newcomer students adjust to school and community life. Nancy is an advocate for the newcomer students and she helps students when they are having trouble with other teachers. You have noticed that Nancy is always running from place to place and at the last staff meeting she started to cry after what seemed like a benign comment.

You teach alongside Nancy and you are worried about her. What can you do?

11. Help from Settlement

You are a settlement worker with a local non-governmental organization. You work with refugee students who have come from war-affected backgrounds. A school has called you to tell you that one of their students is displaying serious anger issues. Yesterday he scratched a girl's face, and the week before he started a fire in the schoolyard. Today, the same boy told another boy that he was coming to school with a knife and he was going to poke the other boy's eyeballs out with it. The school has tried to contact the home, but there has been no reply. As the settlement worker, you know of the family but you do not know the case.

What can you do?

12. Settlement Frustration

You work with a settlement and counselling agency in the inner city, where there is the largest number of refugee families. You work with many schools in the area and you think you are doing excellent partnering and multi-sectoral planning to meet the needs of newcomer youth and families. You know that several students from Margaret Park School are in need of teacher support and if you could just get in to talk to them, everything would be so much better. Students are frustrated and parents from the refugee community feel that the school does not want them. You call the principal several times and leave many messages. You try one last time and are told, "This is a school issue and we can handle it, thank you very much." In other words, please leave us to what we know, we do not need your input. And yet, you know that kids are being excluded and you really want to help.

What do you do? Why might the school be hesitant or reluctant to work with you? What could you do to foster greater cooperation and collaboration with schools, without stepping on toes or crossing boundaries?

13. Child Arrival

A new student from Syria has joined your grade 6 class. The student has had limited schooling and has said very little to you in the last several weeks. When you speak with him one on one, he seems quite reluctant to discuss personal issues, yet he does tell you he is having an ok time in Canada and there are no problems at home or school. His academic level is low and you sense he is at least a few years behind his peers. You don't know why, but you feel that something else is going on with this young boy. You do not have any way of diagnosing or testing him, and you have limited background on the family. You look in his pupil file and see sparse background information.

What can you do?

14. Or Else

The president of the parent council has come in with a petition signed by more than 75 parents demanding that more be done to protect and care for Canadian-born students. Over the past few months there have been several incidents involving several new Syrian students. The incidents include violence against Canadian students, bullying behaviour toward Canadian children, and at least two cases of Syrian children starting physical fights with Canadian children after school. Parents are now demanding that the school put policies and practices in place to protect children. The parents have given the administrator a week to solve this or they are going to the media with documented cases involving their children. You also know that two Syrian children have complained to teachers recently about Canadian children calling them terrorists and accusing them of forcing their values on Canadian kids. As the principal, you sense there is more to this story than meets the eye, but these parents are demanding prompt action.

This whole situation could escalate very quickly and you are worried about how this could affect the staff and students at you school. What will you do?

15. Where to Go
Some of the Muslim students have approached you, their teacher, about their need for a place to pray during the school day. You take their request to your principal who tells you that your job is to teach the curriculum, not promote faith-based practices. You feel stuck knowing that these children need a quiet time and place in to stay true to their religious beliefs. The principal does not seem willing to budge, or even to talk about the issue.

What can you do as a teacher? Why might the principal not want to enter into a discussion about this?

16. Marginalized
The counsellor in your school has been the primary confidante for many of the refugee students. As a teacher of many of the newcomer students, you keep hearing that they are being steered away from any type of post-secondary education and instead being advised to apply for entry-level jobs exclusively. You think it is a huge mistake to provide students with such limited career and educational advice, but you worry about interfering with another professional's role. You have personally taught some of these students and you know they have higher aspirations and the academic ability to handle so much more.

The counsellor is very experienced and tends to be headstrong in her opinions. What can you do?

17. You're Expecting
Tomorrow at 9 am, your elementary school will be receiving three new families from Syria. You are the principal these are the students joining your school: two children, ages 6 and 7, from one family; one child, age 9, and twins, age 10, from another family; and five children—ages 5, 7, 9, 10, and 12—from the third family. You have been told that one of the children in family number 3 is profoundly hearing impaired as a result of an explosion that killed his mother. You are absolutely shocked and have no idea how to go about informing your already overstressed teachers of the new additions to the school just two weeks before Christmas break.

What can you do?

18. Go Home
You are a teacher in a high school and several Muslim students who are very upset have come to you. Over the last few months, each of them has encountered racism in the community. Adults and students have yelled or called out to them, saying they should go back where they came from or calling them terrorists. In addition, several females have felt threatened and upset by males who have told them to remove their hijabs and to start "acting like Canadians." All students are visibly upset and feel unwelcome in Canada. You are worried that some of the students might decide to take matters into their own hands if nothing is done.

What can you do?

19. Help

A mother is sitting in your counselling office and obviously in crisis. She is crying and swearing and tells you that she cannot control her children. She has three girls, ages 9, 11 and 14. The girls do not respect her and will not listen to her. The two oldest want to hang out late at night in the mall and on the street. The mother knows this is unsafe, but her children will not listen. Since they came to Canada, the girls learned in school that parents cannot hit their children. The mother says that when she tries to discipline them they say they do not need to listen to her and there is nothing she can do about it because if she does, they will call CFS to take them away to another home. The mother feels like she has lost control. She is desperate not to lose her children. Her husband left her two months ago when she started working in her first job. He did not feel that his wife should be working, and the conflict resulted in him leaving. The mother has limited English skills but her children have acquired the language quickly, and she feels they purposely speak in English around her so that she cannot understand them.

How can you help this mother?

20. Line Up

A student arrived a year ago from Bhutan. After a year of EAL support and limited progress in English language proficiency, his homeroom teacher feels that he is not capable of the academic work expected in grade 7. The teacher has tried making accommodations in the assessment of the student's learning, but has still not seen evidence that the student is making progress. You are worried that something else is at play. The teacher refers the student to the school-based student services team, who place him on a priority list for a psycho-educational assessment. The teacher has been told that the wait time is a minimum of 3 years and there is no chance of the assessment taking place prior to the student starting high school. The teacher realizes that something has to be done in order to give this student any chance of success, but has no idea where to turn.

What would you tell this teacher to do?

TEACHER LESSON 12: ACADEMIC CULTURE SHOCK

Objectives	Recognize the impact of culture in the classroom and its effect on academic success
Themes	**THEME 4:** Refugee Characteristics **THEME 4d:** Who is the E/FAL Student? **THEME 3b:** Equity
Standards and Guidelines **Competency Areas**	C2.1: Respect Diversity
Materials	• "Academic Culture Shock" by Kara A. Godwin, *New England Journal of Higher Education*, Vol. 13, No. 5 (Spring 2009), p. 30: www.nebhe.org/info/journal/issues/NEJHE_Spring09.pdf

ANTICIPATORY SET:
- Participants should read the article before the session.

ACTIVATION:
- Discussion questions:
  - This article discusses university students. What similarities do you see between them and students in the K–12 school system?
  - What are some differences between university and K–12 students?

ACQUISITION:
- Review the content of the article, focusing on general differences in the classroom cultures of different countries and the impact of different approaches to teaching and learning on students.

- Add to the information in the article by asking:
  - What are some differences in learning styles acceptable in other countries?
  - What role might interrupted learning play in academic culture shock? What student behaviours might indicate academic culture shock based on interrupted learning?
  - What role might social norms play in academic culture shock? What are some of the hidden social norms in the classroom?
  - How might trauma, fear, and anxiety affect academic culture shock? How might these factors be displayed in the classroom setting?

APPLICATION:
- Participants work in small groups to share ideas and ways they can address academic culture shock in their classrooms. Small groups share their ideas with the larger group.

- Scenario: Student in class won't make eye contact with the teacher or raise his/her hand to answer or ask a question.
    - Why might this be the case?
    - What are some strategies for engaging this learner in your classroom?

- Scenario: Student is perpetually tardy for class without reason and refuses to attempt assigned work.
    - Why might this be the case?
    - What are some strategies for engaging this learner in your classroom?

ASSESSMENT:

- Have participants list strategies to integrate students to the classroom culture. If they feel comfortable doing so, participants can share their ideas with the large group or table group.

TEACHER LESSON 13: CULTURAL TOKENISM VERSUS DIVERSITY

Objectives	Recognize cultural diversity to minimize misunderstanding
Themes	**THEME 4:** Refugee Characteristics **THEME 5:** Building Personal and Community Connections
Standards and Guidelines **Competency Areas**	C2.1: Respect Diversity C4.1: Refer Clients to the Appropriate Sources
Materials	• What it's like to be a refugee student in a Canadian classroom (CBC Radio, Tapestry, October 2, 2016, video): http://www.cbc.ca/radio/tapestry/away-from-home-1.3785730/what-it-s-like-to-be-a-refugee-student-in-a-canadian-classroom-1.3785764 • "Diversity in Public Education: Acknowledging Immigrant Parent Knowledge" by Yan Guo, *Canadian Journal of Education*, Vol. 35, No. 2, 2001, pp. 120–140: http://journals.sfu.ca/cje/index.php/cje-rce/article/viewFile/560/1265

ANTICIPATORY SET:

• Have participants read the article from the *Canadian Journal of Education* prior to the session.

• Invite participants to share experiences or known examples of cultural misunderstandings in the classroom.

ACTIVATION:

• View the short video narrated by Dr. Kristiina Montero on the website of the CBC Radio show Tapestry: http://www.cbc.ca/radio/tapestry/away-from-home-1.3785730/what-it-s-like-to-be-a-refugee-student-in-a-canadian-classroom-1.3785764

• Discussion questions:
   • One thing we can take from the video is that the refugee student simply wants you to know what happened with him/her. From that perspective, how could you approach refugee students in the classroom?
   • What are the dangers of generalizing approaches—of using the same approaches with everyone — without considering specific contexts? What considerations are required?
   • How can teachers support non-newcomer/non-refugee students in cultural understanding?

ACQUISITION:

• Review the content of the article, including how others not understanding their cultural practices impacts students, and misconceptions/perceptions of parental involvement that do not fit Eurocentric norms.

APPLICATION:

- Consider the following:
    - It is difficult to know the cultural background of all the students in a class, and to anticipate all the questions and situations that may arise. How can you as a classroom teacher prepare for and address the diversity of your students?
    - Traditional models of parental involvement tend to best serve and reflect White middle-class parents, not the parents of immigrants, or refugees, or from minority backgrounds. Sometimes newcomer parents are engaged in their children's education, but often not in a manner recognized by teachers and administrators. Have you encountered such situations? Describe challenges and successes.

- Have a group conversation on the following questions:
    - As a teacher or settlement worker, how can you access the strength and the wealth of knowledge parents have to help students succeed?
    - What role can parents play in their children's education?
    - What role can culture play in students' education?
    - What role can translators or cultural brokers play in this field?
    - What role can the school staff play in students' education?

- Ask: Moving forward, what changes will you make in your classroom or practices to help incorporate these concepts for inclusion? Have participants share their ideas within a smaller group or with the larger group.

ASSESSMENT:

- Participants can share strategies that they hope to incorporate into their class/school with the larger group.

TEACHER LESSON 14: INTERRUPTED LEARNING

Objectives	Understand and make accommodations for the effects of interrupted learning on the success and well-being of refugee and newcomer students
Themes	**THEME 4d:** Who is the E/FAL Student? **THEME 3b:** Equity
Standards and Guidelines **Competency Areas**	C2.1: Respect Diversity
Materials	• Icosahedron templates (pp. 96-98) photocopied on regular paper • Build a 3-D Icosahedron (p. 95) • Scissors • Glue sticks • Masking tape • Small paper clips

ANTICIPATORY SET:

- As a large group, identify potential barriers to learning caused by "gaps" in education, or interrupted learning. Compile a list of these gaps on the board.

- How might language contribute to gaps? (Encourage responses—there are no wrong answers.)

ACTIVATION:

- Divide participants into 3 groups. Further divide each group into subgroups of no more than 4 to share tools.

- Introduce the main groups as follows:
    - Group 1 are supported learners
    - Group 2 have experienced some interruptions in learning (and have some language acquisition)
    - Group 3 have experienced significant interruptions in learning (and have little language acquisition)

- Make the following things clear to all:
    - There should be no interaction between the numbered groups (1, 2, 3). Groups should not see the templates used by other groups.
    - Participants cannot use phones, laptops, tablets, or other electronic devices.

- All subgroups will now build a 3-D icosahedron. They will receive the same instructions but different tools.

- Group 1 subgroups receive template 1, scissors, glue, and paper clips.
- Group 2 subgroups receive template 2, scissors, and masking tape.
- Group 3 subgroups receive template 3 and masking tape.

- Allow 15–20 minutes for groups to build their icosahedron.

- Optional addition: Have 1–4 participants play the role of teacher. Do not provide them with any additional information. Look for feedback as to how they tried to help, whether or not they were successful, and why or why not.

ACQUISITION:

- Have subgroups share completed icosahedrons within their group and discuss the experience.

- Identify themes within the group that can be shared with the class.

- Have participants verbalize their thoughts about the experience of other groups. Is there empathy, bitterness, confusion, etc.?

APPLICATION:

- Each group received different tools and a different template to which the instructions applied. Mix participants from each group into new subgroups of 4 to discuss:
  1. What skills and/or experience might each of the tools represent?
  2. How might you present the same activity—create an icosahedron—to students in such a way that they all have an opportunity to complete it successfully?
  3. What are some strategies you can use in your classroom to accommodate students with interrupted learning and less language acquisition?
  4. What additional resources and/or supports might be available to you?
  5. What skills, ideas, and values might students bring to the class if they do not have schooling but do have work experience? Explain.

- Have subgroups share their thoughts with the whole group at the end.

ASSESSMENT:

- Have participants design and submit an activity with multi-layered accommodations. Or, if there is little time available, provide a lesson and have participants suggest accommodations.

BUILD A 3-D ICOSAHEDRON

1. Cut along the outside lines of the pattern.

2. Fold the solid lines backward.

3. Glue along the tab sections to secure your shape.

4. Paper clips can be used to support glued sections while the shape is being manipulated.

BUILD A 3-D ICOSAHEDRON

1. Cut along the outside lines of the pattern.

2. Fold the solid lines backward.

3. Glue along the tab sections to secure your shape.

4. Paper clips can be used to support glued sections while the shape is being manipulated.

BUILD A 3-D ICOSAHEDRON

1. Cut along the outside lines of the pattern.

2. Fold the solid lines backward.

3. Glue along the tab sections to secure your shape.

4. Paper clips can be used to support glued sections while the shape is being manipulated.

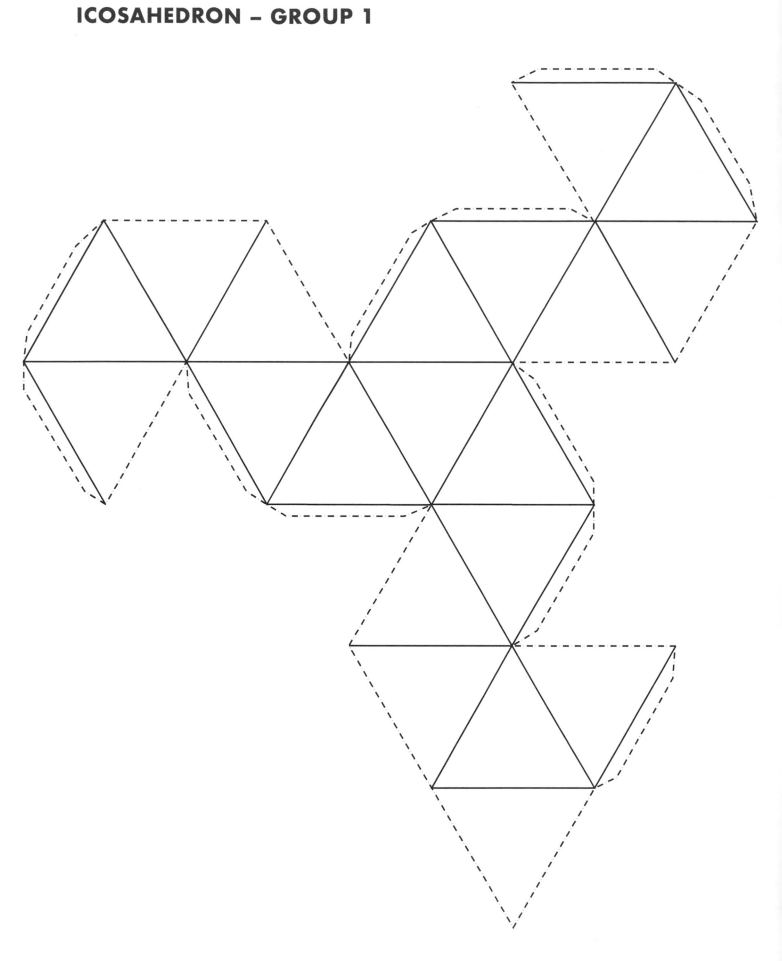

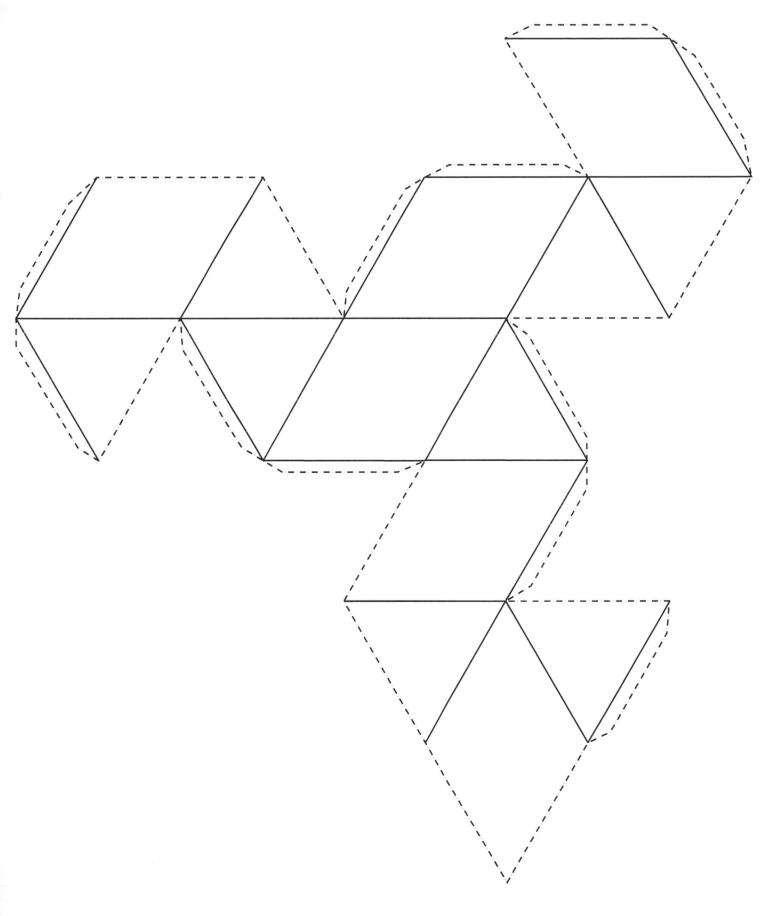

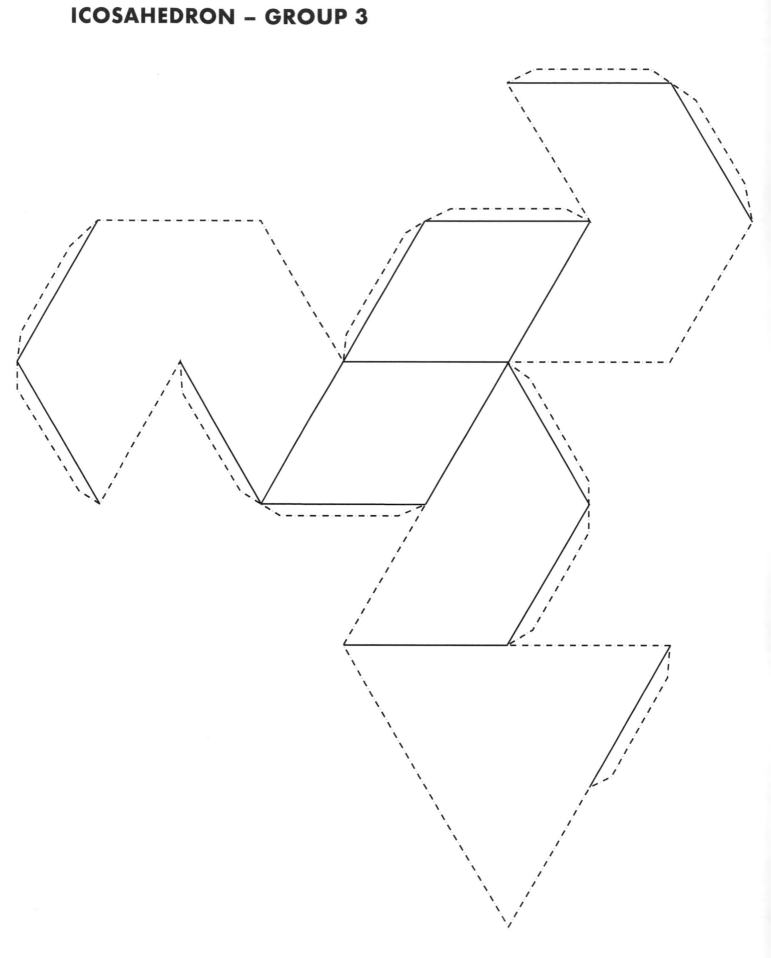

TEACHER LESSON 15: REFRAMING ANGER AND LISTENING REFLECTIVELY

Objectives	Identify sources of anger and strategies to reduce negative behaviours
Themes	**THEME 4a:** Anger **THEME 3a:** Restorative Practices and Justice
Standards and Guidelines **Competency Areas**	C2.3: Develop Productive Interactions with Clients
Materials	• Paper and pens/pencils

ANTICIPATORY SET:

- Say: It is important to be able to "reframe" anger. Think about what else you might call it when you see a student "angry."
    - Is it frustration?
    - Is it anxiety?
    - Is it sadness?

  It is important to recognize these distinct emotions early and respond to them, rather than wait until a student expresses anger or loses self-control.

ACTIVATION:

- Ask participants to think back to the last time they felt angry as a result of something or someone.
    - What was the situation? What other feelings and sensations were running through your body at the time?
    - Did anyone try to help or talk to you? What did they do or say?
    - Would it have made you angrier if someone had tried to intervene by responding only to your anger rather than to the reason you were angry? (Students feel the same way, in that they want you to understand what is going on for them, not simply see and react to their anger.)

ACQUISITION:

- Ask participants to think again about that time they were angry. Ask: Was there another emotion that you also felt? What if, instead of calling what you felt "anger," you called it the other emotion (be it frustration, anxiety, sadness, or something else)?

- If we reframe anger and call it the emotion that is behind/beneath it, "anger management" becomes managing those other emotions first. Children and youth often don't understand those behind-the-scenes emotions. Teachers and caregivers can help young people make sense of all of their emotions and identify the foundation or source of any anger. The goal is to empower students to manage their primary emotions. If it is possible to intervene early and to help a student identify and manage his or her emotions, outbursts may be avoided. As a child's teacher, you will be able to notice when the child needs some re-direction or a break.

- Ask participants to read the following statements and identify an emotion, other than anger, that may help to explain how a student is feeling. (You can help a student reframe the situation by making a suggestion, e.g., "Maybe you're feeling _____" or "Perhaps you are feeling _____ because _____. Do you need a break?")
    - "I don't want to present this to the class! This is so stupid!"
    - "Get away from me! Leave me alone!"
    - "I don't want to wait in this **** lineup."
    - "Fine then. You obviously don't want me in this class! I'm leaving!"

- As a group, discuss each situation and compare the emotions different participants associated with each scenarios. Possible prompts:
    - How might you respond differently to each situation if you don't think of the student as being "angry"?
    - How would a student respond if you immediately assume they are about to have an angry outburst that needs to be "managed"?
    - Anger carries certain connotations with it. How does reframing anger help to build empathy and understanding?
    - How might helping a student to identify their emotions help them to feel more in control? How would it help a student save face?

APPLICATION:

- Present and discuss the following plan to help students reframe anger:
    - Have students create a personalized chart or mind map of what happens in their bodies before an angry outburst. They can write or draw what they feel. For example:
        - Grumpy
        - Sweaty palms
        - Racing heart
        - Frustrated
        - Clenched jaw or hands (tight muscles)
        - Red face
        - Not wanting to talk to anyone
        - Feeling like if I talk, 'If I talk, I'm going to say something mean'

    - Next, have students write situations that lead to angry outbursts. Examples:
        - Sitting in class for too long
        - Having to wait in line
        - Having to wait with my hand up before the teacher can help me with a task
        - Being nagged or bothered by a friend or classmate
        - Feeling like my friends, teachers, or classmates aren't listening to me
        - Having a bad morning at home before school
        - Not getting to have breakfast

    - Next, have students "reframe" their anger. Beside each situation, have them write an emotion, other than anger, that describes how they feel.

- Finally, have students write or draw calming techniques that work or that they are willing to try the next time they are in a situation that triggers anger. Examples:
    - Deep breathing
    - Leave classroom and go for a walk
    - Use a grounding technique (identify something you can hear, smell, taste, feel and see).
    - Repeat a mantra to yourself like "Be calm. You are strong."
    - Do something physical like jumping jacks, running on the spot, etc.

- In future, after an angry outburst or situation that leaves a student feeling angry, have the student reflect on what happened using their chart/map and these ideas. The more students identify and reframe their feelings, the more adeptly they will be able to respond to those feelings and use techniques to calm themselves.

- Discussion questions:
    - What challenges do you anticipate in applying these strategies to the classroom?
    - Which emotions are likely to be easily identified by students? Which might be more difficult to identify?
    - What other strategies could assist students in identifying the foundations of their anger?

ASSESSMENT:

- Ask participants to write down strategies that can be applied in different situations. If they feel comfortable doing so, participants can share their ideas with the large group or table group.

TEACHER LESSON 16: COLLABORATION BETWEEN E/FAL AND SUBJECT-AREA TEACHERS

Objectives	Extend knowledge of collaborative teaching and learning techniques for students acquiring a new language
Themes	**THEME 5:** Building Personal and Community Connections **THEME 3b:** Equity
Standards and Guidelines Competency Areas	C4.1: Refer Clients to the Appropriate Sources C3.1: Possess Career Development Knowledge
Materials	• "Collaboration Between ESL and Content Teachers: How Do We Know When We Are Doing It Right?" by Chris Davison, *International Journal of Bilingual Education and Bilingualism*, Vol. 9, No. 4, pp. 454–475: https://www.researchgate.net/publication/254242346_Collaboration_Between_ESL_and_Content_Teachers_How_Do_We_Know_When_We_Are_Doing_It_Right

ANTICIPATORY SET:
- Participants should read the article prior to the session. Questions to consider:
    - What is collaborative learning/teaching?
    - What are the linguistic demands on learners/teachers in the subject area classroom?

ACTIVATION:
- Display the following continuum:

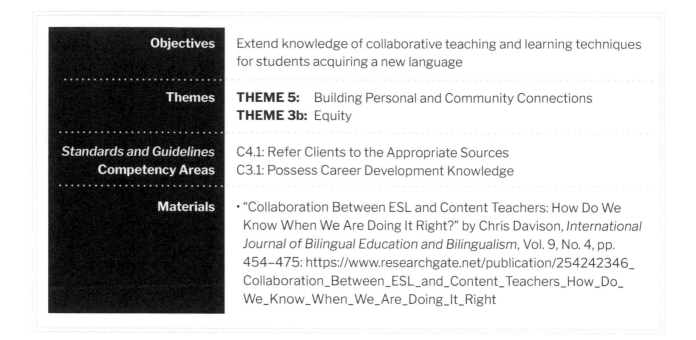

Pseudo-compliance or passive resistance → Compliance – Accommodation → Convergence (and some co-option) → Creative co-construction

- Discussion questions:
    - Where on the continuum do you rate yourself in collaborating with another teacher? Why?
    - What are some strategies that your school is currently implementing to ensure there is collaboration between E/FAL teachers and subject-area teachers?
    - What are some barriers to collaboration in your teaching situation? How might these be overcome?
    - What supports can you use to improve or create a space for collaboration?

ACQUISITION:
- Review material in the article, including:
    - Relevance of teacher/classroom collaboration
    - Stages of collaboration
    - Framework for collaboration
    - Examples of effective collaboration

APPLICATION:

- Working in groups, participants strategize ways that E/FAL and subject-area teachers can work together to support and encourage students as well as each other.
    - Groups compile a list of strategies that is shared with the larger group.
    - Groups are encouraged to think of sample activities to share with the larger group.

- Groups share their ideas with the larger group and the information is summarized on the board.

ASSESSMENT:

- Ask participants to share one idea from the list that they will take back to their schools to implement.

TEACHER LESSON 17: HOW DIVERSE IS YOUR WORLD?

This lesson is an adaption of "Diversity in Your Life," from *Cultural Proficiency: A Manual for School Leaders* by Randall B. Lindsey, Kikanza Nuri Robins, and Raymond D. Terrell (Thousand Oaks, CA: Corwin, 2009), pp. 170–171.

Objectives	Recognize cultural blind spots to consider needs of culturally diverse students
Themes	**THEME 5:** Building Personal and Community Connections **THEME 6:** Cultural Competency/Culturally Responsive Teaching
Standards and Guidelines **Competency Areas**	C2.1: Respect Diversity C4.1: Refer Clients to the Appropriate Sources
Materials	• Many beads in 8 different colours (**Note:** You will need enough beads per colour for each question—see below. If you don't have or want to use beads, the alternative approach included below requires only chart paper and markers.) • Clear plastic cups (one per person) • Paper and pens/pencils

ANTICIPATORY SET:

- To prepare for the session, collect beads in 8 different colours and assign a different colour to each of the following categories:
    - European, American, Canadian
    - African, Black American, Black Canadian
    - Asian, Pacific Islander
    - Latino, Hispanic
    - Biracial
    - Indigenous, First Nations, Aboriginal
    - Gay, Lesbian, Bisexual, Transgendered, Two-Spirited
    - Physically or Mentally Disabled

    Post the list of what each bead colour represents where participants will be able to see it.

- To begin, ask participants: Do you interact with people of different cultures? Different races? Allow participants a few minutes to reflect on this question and to free-write a journal response. Emphasize that the information is for personal growth and will be kept private.

- Tell participants you are now going to examine the diversity of the people they encounter in their daily life.

ACTIVATION:

- Give each person an empty cup and point to the list of what each bead colour represents.

- Explain that you will now ask participants to select beads that most closely represent certain people they know and come into contact with.

Alternative approach:

- Write each category/group (biracial, Asian/Pacific Islander, etc.) on a separate sheet of chart paper. Post the sheets around the room with a marker at each one.

- As you ask the questions, participants move to the appropriate sheet of paper and add a tick mark. Pause after each question for participants to survey the room and the other sheets.

- Afterward, tally the ticks on each sheet of chart paper and compile the total for each on the board.

- Discuss the tallied results.

ACQUISITION:

- Read the following to the group and have participants pick an appropriately coloured bead for each answer.

Select a bead the most closely represents...

1. you
2. your partner/significant other or your family (if you do not have a partner/significant other)
3. your closest friend
4. your boss
5. your neighbour
6. your doctor
7. your dentist
8. your mechanic
9. your lawyer
10. your spiritual leader
11. your co-workers, predominately
12. the people in the last movie you say, predominantly
13. the people in your favourite TV show
14. the person you most admire
15. the people in your favourite music group/band
16. the people with whom you come in contact during a typical day, predominantly
17. the people in your social circle, predominantly
18. your professors/teachers, past or present
19. the majority of the people at your favourite hangout spot or social club
20. your favourite actress/actor

APPLICATION:

- Have participants hold their cups up so that everyone can see. Ask them to look around the room.

- Post the following questions on the board:
    1. What do you notice?
    2. How diverse is your world?
    3. How does it compare to the world of others?
    4. Is it dominated by one group? Could this change? Do you want to change this?

- Discuss the above questions at table groups before discussing the findings as a large group.

- Use these questions to reflect on the activity as a whole:
    - Why did we do this activity?
    - How could we adapt this activity?
    - What did you learn about yourself through this activity?

ASSESSMENT:

- Invite participants to submit a short exit slip reflecting on what it was like to do this activity and what they learned, both about themselves and others.

TEACHER LESSON 18: DEFINING AND UNDERSTANDING CULTURE

This lesson is an adaption of "Who Are You?" from *Cultural Proficiency: A Manual for School Leaders* by Randall B. Lindsey, Kikanza Nuri Robins, and Raymond D. Terrell (Thousand Oaks, CA: Corwin, 2009), pp. 188–189.

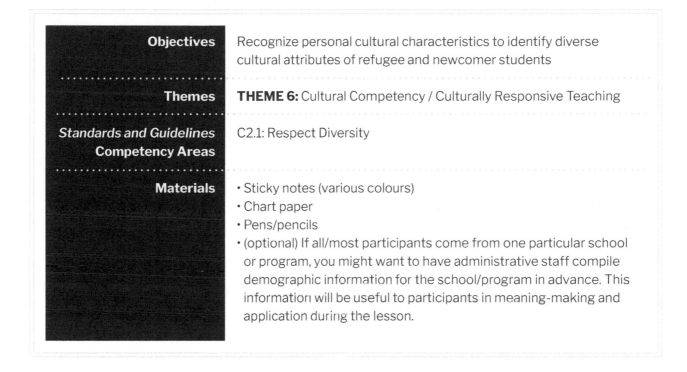

Objectives	Recognize personal cultural characteristics to identify diverse cultural attributes of refugee and newcomer students
Themes	**THEME 6:** Cultural Competency / Culturally Responsive Teaching
***Standards and Guidelines* Competency Areas**	C2.1: Respect Diversity
Materials	• Sticky notes (various colours) • Chart paper • Pens/pencils • (optional) If all/most participants come from one particular school or program, you might want to have administrative staff compile demographic information for the school/program in advance. This information will be useful to participants in meaning-making and application during the lesson.

ANTICIPATORY SET:

- Ask "Who are you?" 10 times. Each time you ask the question, participants write a response on a sticky note.
  - Participants should try to create 10 different statements about who they are.
  - There should be no talking among participants, and participants should be told that this information will not be shared with the group; it will be kept private.

- Debrief the activity by asking the following:
  - What did you notice as you wrote your list?
  - What did you learn about yourself?
  - Why do you think we did this exercise?

ACTIVATION:

- Ask: What does culture mean to you? Allow time for participants to think about this question and write an individual response on a sticky note.

- Next, ask: "What are some characteristics of culture?" Again, allow time for participants to reflect on the question and record characteristics on sticky notes. (Participants will now have several completed sticky notes.)

- After about 5 minutes, ask participants to pair up and compare responses. Ask pairs to sort all of their sticky notes into two piles: characteristics of culture that are visible and characteristics that are not always visible.

- Ask participants to create one or two statements about the clustering of their sticky notes. What stands out? How can the two groupings be summarized? Participants should be prepared to share their summaries with the larger group.

ACQUISITION:
Part 1:
- Ask table groups to list personal cultural characteristics on sticky notes (specific food preferences, clothing, rituals, religion, language, non-verbal communication, etc.).

- Draw a T-chart on chart paper. Invite participants to place their sticky notes with personal characteristics on the left-hand side of the T-chart, and have them add behaviours associated with each characteristic on the right-hand side.

- Have participants identify which behaviours are personally acceptable and not acceptable to them (e.g., non-verbal eye contact or lack of eye contact). Then, generate a list of what Canadians deem acceptable and not acceptable in their broader culture. Compare and contrast what is acceptable to individuals with what is acceptable more widely.

APPLICATION:
Part 2:
- Pose the following four questions to the table groups and have each group create responses to the questions using chart paper. Responses will be shared back with the larger group and compiled. This is where demographic information about the program/school, if you have it, can be shared and referred to:
  - Which cultural groups live within the service area of your program/school?
  - What do you know about the lifestyle, immigration history, health beliefs, communication style, etc. of each cultural group? What do you need to still learn about? Where could you learn about this cultural framework?
  - What do you know about the different ideas for raising children held within these cultural groups? How might this impact a parent's connection to your program/school?
  - How did you learn this culturally based information?

- Responses are some examples of components of cultural frameworks. Discuss why it is important to not make assumptions based on culture.

Optional extension activities:
- Ask participants to build a cultural profile of their school or community in addition to researching cultural background information for the above four questions.

- Invite a cultural broker (or multiple cultural brokers) to present to the group about different cultures represented in their schools/community.

ASSESSMENT:

- Participants discuss their answers to the application questions at their table groups. Collect feedback during the large-group discussions and debrief after the activity.

- Remind participants that there are differing values, customs, and beliefs within any culture. Diversity within cultures exists, and it is important that educators do not make assumptions based on incomplete information or cultural assumptions.

TEACHER LESSON 19: BASIC COUNSELLING SKILL – ACTIVE LISTENING

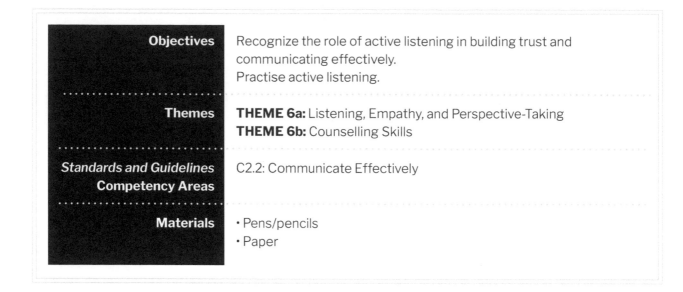

Objectives	Recognize the role of active listening in building trust and communicating effectively. Practise active listening.
Themes	**THEME 6a:** Listening, Empathy, and Perspective-Taking **THEME 6b:** Counselling Skills
***Standards and Guidelines* Competency Areas**	C2.2: Communicate Effectively
Materials	• Pens/pencils • Paper

Teachers have many responsibilities beyond teaching curriculum. For some students, reaching out is taking a chance, and how the person they reach out to reacts is vital. Teachers may only get one shot to get it right! This lesson emphasizes the importance of listening, even amidst the business of the day.

ACTIVATION:

- Divide participants into groups of 3. It is most effective if participants are grouped with people they don't know well and groups are spread out as much as possible.

- Within each group, participants establish a Listener, a Speaker, and an Observer.

- Ask the Listeners to step outside. Explain the other roles as follows:
    - **Speakers** – You will talk to your group about an important life experience you have had. Share your excitement, sadness, worry, etc. but stay in your comfort zone!
    - **Observers** – You will watch the others in your group. Pay attention to how each individual behaves. Be prepared to offer anecdotal observations to the class.

- Explain to the Listeners their role outside the room (out of earshot of the Speakers and Observers).
    - **Listeners** – While the speaker is telling you about their experience, you will remain distracted (try not to be too obvious). You will make little eye contact, just enough to have them think it's okay to continue. Use props (paper, phone, etc.) to divert attention.

ACQUISITION:

- Bring everyone back together and have them begin the activity. Allow approximately 5 minutes for the activity; walk around the room making your own observations throughout. When the time has elapsed, bring the entire group back together to discuss and debrief about the activity.

APPLICATION:

- Allow a few moments for open discussion and settling. Debrief, using the following guided questions for reference, and note the reactions and emotions of speakers and observers on the board or on poster paper:

Speakers
- Describe your experience.
- How did the activity make you feel?
- Did you continue to tell your story or stop talking?

Observers
- Describe your experience.
- What did you notice during the activity?
- How did you feel as a bystander?
- Did you step in to pick up the conversation?

Listeners
- Describe your experience.
- How did your role in the activity make you feel?
- What response did you get from your group?

- Close with discussion around the importance of active and attentive listening, especially by teachers.

    - Trust is precious. Offering undivided attention to someone who has placed their trust in you can be a critical moment in their lives.
    - Listening attentively means putting everything aside and being wholly present with an individual in the moment. If this is not possible, sincerely express the desire to listen and make arrangements to do so at another time. **Be sure to follow through!**
    - One of the biggest dangers of not taking the time to actively listen is that the student will not try again and will continue to struggle and/or internalize matters.
    - Teachers must be willing to recognize when it is time be an empathic listener and when it is time to refer to appropriate resources.
    - It is not within everyone to be comfortable hearing about emotional or traumatic issues. **This is okay!** A good relationship will often allow for a "transfer of trust" to an appropriate person or resource.

ASSESSMENT:

- Ask participants to write a reflection that describes a time when they did not feel heard or understood or a time when they did not listen or misunderstood someone else. What did that feel like? What happened? How could active listening have altered their experience?

TEACHER LESSON 20: BASIC COUNSELLING SKILL – ATTENDING

Objectives	Identify and apply the counselling skill of attending in the regular
Themes	**THEME 6b:** Counselling Skills **THEME 6a:** Listening, Empathy, and Perspective-Taking
Standards and Guidelines **Competency Areas**	C2.2: Communicate Effectively
Materials	• none

Effective listening is very important when providing support to students in need. Effective listening doesn't only give students the opportunity to tell their stories, it validates their experiences. Attending refers to multiple key factors in effective listening including body language/positioning, eye contact, and tone of voice.

Although the stories shared during this lesson will be light and generic, it is still important to establish among the group that personal information is confidential and to be respected.

ACTIVATION:

- Distribute participants around the room in groups of 3 (preferably participants who do not know one another). Identify a speaker, listener, and observer to start (roles will rotate). The roles of each person throughout the exercises are as follows:
  - **Speaker** – Will speak to the listener about something of their choice (e.g., weekend experience, upcoming event, pet, visit with friend/relative).
  - **Listener** – Will listen and respond to speaker.
  - **Observer** – Will observe conversation and interaction in general and provide feedback. Take notes.

- It is important that participants rotate through the roles in the same order in each round (i.e., each speaker has the same listener and observer) so that participants can reflect on differences and changes in the experience.

- Begin Round 1. Each person takes a turn in each role, speaking about themselves or an experience as mentioned above. Allow 5 minutes for each conversation then transition to a new speaker.

- After 15 minutes, when everyone has had an opportunity in each role, come back as a group. The facilitator shares observations and asks how the experience was for everyone. Did listeners feel they had clarity? Did speakers feel heard? Did observers sense some level of comfort in both the speaker and listener?

ACQUISITION:

- How helpers respond, not only with their words but with their bodies, can have a tremendous impact on the comfort and validation of the one telling their story or seeking assistance. In Round 2, participants will practise an awareness of body language by positioning themselves comfortably opposite or alongside the speaker. (It's okay to ask the speaker where they prefer you to sit). Share the following suggestions and techniques for listeners with all participants.

  - Pay attention to posture, try to stay on the same level as your speaker, possibly leaning in to give your undivided attention. Be sure to take non-verbal cues from the speaker as well (e.g., if the listener leans in and the speaker leans back, the listener should pull back a bit to give the speaker space). Eye contact is another way we show undivided attention. Be mindful of cultural and/or social sensitivities around eye contact as it can be interpreted as disrespectful and/or intimidating. When appropriate, maintain eye contact with the speaker or position yourself alongside them, angled slightly in their direction.

  - Responding to the speaker by summarizing and paraphrasing what they have said not only confirms that they have been heard, it also allows the listener to ensure they have understood correctly (giving opportunity for corrections) and to ask questions for further inquiry. Use statements such as
    - What I hear you saying is...
    - It sounds like
    - Help me understand...
    - Let me see if I have this....

  - These techniques can feel awkward at first, especially if participants are overthinking them. With time and practise, they will become more natural and habitual.

  - It is important not to make assumptions or infer thoughts, feelings, experiences, or responses that have not been stated. Do not add or embellish a speaker's story or attempt to be a problem solver—simply listen and request clarification as needed.

APPLICATION:

- Time to practise! In their original groups, participants complete a second round of 5-minute sessions to practise attending and responding. The speakers will choose a different topic than in Round 1. (Remind participants to rotate through the roles in the same order, so that each speaker has the same listener and observer.) The observer plays an important role here, making notes of the interactions as well as observable differences from Round 1.

- Debrief at the end of Round 2 for differences in each role. Speakers should have felt a more significant presence of their listener and listeners should have noticed greater clarity and response from their speaker. Allow observers to offer constructive feedback about things they may have noticed that can be practised in the future.

ASSESSMENT:

- Ask participants to write down some of the things they have learned and how these can be applied in different situations. If they feel comfortable doing so, participants can share their ideas with the large group or table group.

TEACHER LESSON 21: CLASSROOM STRATEGIES AND BEST PRACTICES

Objectives	Increase knowledge of classroom strategies and practices for supporting refugee and newcomer students
Themes	**THEME 6:** Cultural Competency/Culturally Safe and Responsive Teaching
Standards and Guidelines **Competency Areas**	C2.3: Develop Productive Interactions with Clients

Materials	• "Classroom Strategies" in *Meeting the Needs of Students from Diverse Cultures: A Handbook for Administrators* by the Department of Education, Newfoundland and Labrador, 2010, pp. 12–13: http://www.ed.gov.nl.ca/edu/k12/curriculum/guides/esl/Meeting-the-Needs.pdf
	• Tips for teachers in 5 key areas (TeachingRefugees.com, Calgary Board of Education, 2014):
	    • Create Safety and Routines: http://teachingrefugees.com/wp-content/uploads/2014/02/Create-Safety-and-Routines-Tips-for-Teachers.pdf
	    • Build Connections
	    • Foster Emotional Skills
	    • Learn When to Refer
	    • Do Self-Care

ANTICIPATORY SET:

- Encourage participants to think about and write down some strategies they currently use in their classroom to support refugee children and youth.

- Participants can review relevant classroom strategies compiled by the Department of Education of Newfoundland and Labrador in Meeting the Needs of Students from Diverse Cultures: A Handbook for Administrators (http://www.ed.gov.nl.ca/edu/k12/curriculum/guides/esl/Meeting-the-Needs.pdf).

ACTIVATION:

- Introduce 5 key areas that teachers need to pay attention to better engage newcomer students in their classroom (as per TeachingRefugees.com):
  - Create safety and routines
  - Build connections
  - Foster emotional skills
  - Do self-care
  - Learn when to refer

- Divide participants into 5 groups and hand out one tip sheet to each group. Participants should review the information provided in the tip sheet, discuss how it does or might apply to their classroom/school, and prepare information on their key area to share with the group.

- After each small group has shared their information, have a large group discussion on the area and note additional ideas and practices shared by other groups.

- After all small groups have presented, ensure everyone gets a copy of all 5 tips sheets.

ACQUISITION:

- Facilitate a group discussion around the challenges that participants might have experienced in their classrooms/schools with refugee and newcomer students. Focus the discussion on the strategies participants have used in the past, or how they hope to deal with difficulties in the future. The goal is for participants, who may have different roles and responsibilities (e.g., teachers, principals, educational assistants, counsellors), to share their knowledge. Assign 1 or 2 note-takers to record ideas and strategies from the discussion to be shared with the group afterward.

APPLICATION:

- Invite a service provider or experienced teacher/professor to talk to the group about strategies they use to support children and youth impacted by conflict.

- Allow participants to ask questions to gather further information on classroom strategies/supports they can take back to their class/school.

ASSESSMENT:

- Ask participants to write down some of the things they have learned and how these can be applied in different situations. If they feel comfortable doing so, participants can share their ideas with the large group or table group.

TEACHER LESSON 22: REFLECTIVE AND MEDITATIVE PAINTING AS A FORM OF STRESS REDUCTION

Objectives	Explore the use of meditative painting to reduce student stress and encourage classroom cohesion
Themes	**THEME 6c:** Expressive Arts **THEME 4b:** Stress
Standards and Guidelines **Competency Areas**	C2.1: Respect Diversity
Materials	• Bristol board, poster board, or canvases • Acrylic paints • Variety of paint brushes, sponges, cloths, and tools for creating effects (combs, feathers, shells, etc.) • Containers of water (to clean brushes) • Rags (to dry brushes and clean up) **Note:** Materials for this lesson are readily found at discount and dollar stores.

ANTICIPATORY SET:

• Relaxation techniques can be learned and experienced in a number of different ways. Open dialogue by discussing different ways participants choose to relax and reflect. What feelings do participants associate with these activities?

• Reassure the group that there are no rules or instructions to follow in this activity. In the paintings they will create, they can use one or many colours and one or many textures. The goal is not the end product but the process of creating a piece that brings calm. This process will look different for everyone.

• A demonstration may encourage freedom and the use of the different utensils. Show participants different strokes such as "dabbing" the brush and smooth swipes, as well as short and long strokes. Demonstrate creating wavy textures using the teeth of a comb.

ACTIVATION:

• Create a calm environment by adjusting light levels and putting on background music (optional).

• The have participants:
   • choose favourite paint colours as well as some they find calming or soothing;
   • choose one or more utensils for applying paint (fingers are also an option);
   • find space to comfortably begin painting.

- Optional: Begin with some deep breathing and/or meditation exercises. (There are several apps available that provide guided breathing and meditations.)

ACQUISITION:

- Have participants begin to apply colour to their board or canvas in whatever form they choose. It's okay if they are tentative to start! Allow for free expression and experimentation with colours and tools.

- Encourage deep breaths throughout the activity.

- Once enough time has passed for participants to settle into their paintings, roam the room, calmly and quietly asking participants how they are connecting and reacting to their work. What are they thinking as they apply the medium? What are they feeling?

- Maintain the calm environment through clean-up (e.g., do not turn on harsh lights, use loud voices, or make excess noise).

APPLICATION:

- Engage in a large-group discussion:
  - What were your thoughts and feelings at the beginning of the exercise?
  - Did these emotions and thoughts change as you painted?
  - What role, if any, did the lighting and/or background music play?

- Talk about how this activity might be used with students:
  - How can this type of activity be used in a classroom setting? Does the activity have to be painting? What elements would be needed to achieve the same effect in a classroom of students (at various ages/stages of development)?
  - How might this type of activity assist refugee and newcomer students? Other students?
  - What advantages and disadvantages do you anticipate with this type of activity?

ASSESSMENT:

- Ask participants to create another expressive arts activity that would benefit all students, regardless of their backgrounds. If they feel comfortable doing so, participants can share their ideas with the large group or table group.

TEACHER LESSON 23: BASIC COUNSELLING SKILL – BUILDING EMPATHY

Objectives	Identify ways in which to enhance classroom-based listening and inclusivity skills
Themes	**THEME 6a:** Listening, Empathy, and Perspective-Taking
Standards and Guidelines **Competency Areas**	C2.2: Communicate Effectively
Materials	• *The Seven Teachings* by David Courchene Jr. (Trafford Publishing, 2007) • Several small- to medium-sized flat rocks with one of the following words (the 7 Sacred Teachings) printed on each one in marker: love, humility, honesty, truth, wisdom, courage, respect • "7" by William Prince, a graduation song written for the Peguis First Nation Class of 2016: https://soundcloud.com/william-prince-music/7a-1 • Paper • Sticky notes • Storybooks (fit the purpose of lesson and grade level)

This lesson can easily be adapted to fit a wide range of themes. The purpose of this particular lesson is to teach participants to listen to other people when they share a personal story. Participants will see and hear how one word can prompt the sharing of many different stories and experiences. Using the 7 Sacred Teachings naturally and authentically embeds character traits as well as Indigenous knowledge and perspectives into the classroom.

ACTIVATION:

- Share this quote by Arthur Mauro: "If we tell each other our stories, we can never again be enemies." Ask participants to turn and talk to the person beside them about what this quote means to them.

- Pile the rocks onto the centre of the table or learning space. Explain that each rock has a different word on it. Each word is one of the 7 Sacred Teachings according to the Ojibwe people: love, humility, honesty, truth, wisdom, courage and respect.
  - Read *The Seven Teachings* by David Courchene Jr. to appreciate the deeper meaning in each individual word. This will help connect the words to space and place.
  - Play "7" by William Prince (https://soundcloud.com/william-prince-music/7a-1), which is a graduation song written for the Peguis First Nation Class of 2016.

- Discuss how these words and their meaning change according to context.

- What comes to mind when you hear the word love? Humility? Honesty? Truth? Wisdom? Courage? Respect?
    - Do these words have the same meaning across cultures?
    - How are different meanings important to learners and teachers?

ACQUISITION:

- Tell the participants that they are now going to focus on ways of listening to other people by sharing a little story about themselves. Refer to the quote mentioned above. The purpose of sharing stories is to build community and empathy by getting to know each other. Using specific words, as they are about to do, increases vocabulary and keeps us rooted to the purpose.

- As a group, create criteria for the audience to follow while each speaker is sharing her/his story. For example: Listeners agree to actively pay attention with all senses. Stories are confidential and cannot be shared without permission.

- Have each participant pick up a rock without looking.

- Based on the context of the group, the purpose, and the time, each participant should share a story that exemplifies the word. For example: "I chose the word courage. When I was 18 years old, instead of going to university like my friends, I packed my bags and flew to Israel to work on a kibbutz. This required courage because I had no friends or family in Israel, I did not speak Hebrew and I travelled alone..."

- Participants can tell their story briefly, share their story in more detail, or write their story on paper. Participants can share stories orally, as a gallery walk, or at small group tables.

APPLICATION:

- Give each participant a few medium-sized sticky notes. For each story they read, view, or listen to, they leave a comment on a sticky note about how that story affected them. For example: "I was affected by your strength and courage. I am not sure I could do what you did. I would love to hear more."

- Discuss with participants how they might adapt this activity for use with students. Depending on age/stage of development and literacy skills, consider using media other than writing to share stories, e.g., drawing or painting, collage or clay, audio or video recording.

Other tools/resources:
- Images to represent each of the 7 Sacred Teachings (to support participants/students with different levels of literacy in English). Samples:
    - https://s-media-cache-ak0.pinimg.com/originals/5b/71/a2/5b71a217c2c92f4f1e248d3c-89c19aae.jpg
    - https://s-media-cache-ak0.pinimg.com/736x/65/02/f1/6502f17c120440f6ba196af-85c7ae669.jpg

- Excellent resource for deepening understanding:
    - The Seven Sacred Teachings of White Buffalo Calf Woman - Niizhwaaswi gagiikwewin. by David Bouchard and Dr. Joseph Martin (Vancouver, BC: More Than Words Publishers, 2009): http://www.btgwinnipeg.ca/uploads/5/2/4/1/52412159/the_seven_sacred_teachings_.pdf

ASSESSMENT:

- Ask participants to write down some of the things they learned and how these can be applied in different situations. If they feel comfortable doing so, participants can share their ideas with the large group or table group.

TEACHER LESSON 24: ARTIFACT STORYTELLING

Objectives	Explore the use of artifact storytelling to connect with students and improve connections between students
Themes	**THEME 6d:** Storytelling **THEME 5:** Building Personal and Community Connections
Standards and Guidelines **Competency Areas**	C2.2 Communicate Effectively
Materials	• Personal artifacts (facilitator and participants) • "Every body has the right… United by Stories": https://vimeo.com/215902063. • Chart paper • Paper • Pencils/pens

ANTICIPATORY SET:

Artifact storytelling involves
- reflecting about your own sense of self,
- listening to others and feeling the courage to share,
- connecting your world with others authentically.

To learn more about artifact storytelling, watch "Every body has the right… United by Stories": https://vimeo.com/215902063.

This lesson also encourages imagining, experimenting with metaphors, and working collaboratively to create a story, product, or simple message.

Before the lesson can begin, you as the facilitator must bring in an object that fits into the palm of your hand and be ready to share a personal story that connects you to this object. A few days before the session, remind participants to bring in their own artifact/object.

ACTIVATION:
- Begin the session by pulling out your object and sharing your story. Keep the object in your hand for all to see as you speak. Example:

I have a tiny toy plastic bike. One of my bike stories is this: I have literally travelled the world with one of my bikes. When I was 19 years old I moved to Germany because I was tired of going to school. I didn't know what I wanted to do at university. I was also tired of being an athlete. I knew I didn't have the money to become a professional triathlete. So, I packed my stuff into a bag and got on a plane. I went to Germany because I have some family there, and when I arrived, I decided to volunteer. So,

I cycled into the town where my family lived, which is also where the top triathlete in Germany also lives. We met and everything changed...

- When you finish telling your story, ask the participants what they learned about you. Jot their thoughts on chart paper.

- Then ask the participants to get into small groups of 4 or 5. During this time, they are to share their own artifacts and connect each artifact to a personal story.

ACQUISITION:

- After all the groups have spent time sharing with each other, ask to borrow 5–7 artifacts. Tell participants that you will start a story a story about building peace and community and they will help you finish it. Tell them that you will be using the artifacts as metaphors. For example, a hockey puck could be the black hole of death. Here is the beginning of a story for the following artifacts: a bike, a flower, a purple gemstone, and a water bottle.

One day, a strange man wearing flowing colourful scarves pulled into town on his bike. The bike had many different decorations including a flower that turned into a speaker phone. He stopped his magical bike, turned on the speaker phone, and said, 'I have a present for the first person to appear in front of my tent at 8 o'clock tonight. All I ask is that you bring your most treasured possession." The townspeople were curious, alarmed, and excited. Everyone spent the day searching and shopping for a treasured possession, in order to get the magical gift. While they searched and shopped high and low, the young child of a single mother walked over to the man on the bike and offered to help set up his tent. He said, 'Child, don't you want to search for the possession you will show me to get my magical gift?" The child replied that she had no money or possession to show off and would rather help set up the tent.

At 8 o'clock that night, everyone from the town showed up with fancy jewels, exotic tools, and new machines that they had spent all day finding, making, and buying.

- Finish the story as a group. To develop the story, you could prompt ideas with the following questions:
    - What happens when the strange man sees all the money and time the townspeople spent acquiring possessions?
    - What is the role of the little girl who has no possessions and only a poor mother as family?
    - How can we use a purple gemstone and a water bottle to complete our story?
    - How will this town become a more peaceful place?

- Identify a key message from the story when it is complete.

- Ask the participants in their small groups to place 5 of their artifacts on the table and to begin writing their own story together.

- Once all the stories have been written, create a space for participants to share their experiences in co-creating. Ask:
    - What was most challenging about the task?
    - What positive experiences occurred during the task? What setbacks?
    - Now that you have attempted the task, how would you adjust your process (if at all)?

APPLICATION:

- Discuss how this creative activity can be used in a classroom setting.
    - What adjustments would be needed for different grade levels?
    - What adjustments could be made for variable literacy levels?
    - What challenges do you foresee? What benefits to you foresee?

ASSESSMENT:

- Ask participants to modify or re-design the lesson for students (at each participant's preferred grade level). If they feel comfortable doing so, participants can share their ideas with the large group or table group.

TEACHER LESSON 25: MATCHING NEEDS TO SERVICES

Objectives	Identify services of assistance to refugee and newcomer students and barriers that may inhibit use
Themes	**THEME 7:** Equity **THEME 2:** Social Determinants of Health
Standards and Guidelines Competency Areas	C3.1: Possess Career Development Knowledge C2.1: Respect Diversity

Materials	• Puzzle Person (p. 127)
	  • photocopies of the whole person on cardstock or other heavy paper
	  • photocopies of the person cut into pieces (body parts) on any type of paper
	• Masking tape
	• Chart paper and markers

ANTICIPATORY SET:

- Facilitate large group discussion on the extended role of the teacher:
    - What types of assistance, outside required classroom duties, should classroom teachers offer/not offer. (Allow for constructive debate.)
    - What are some barriers to services?
    - How might students (and their learning) be affected if the needs of the immediate family are not met in the community? If the needs of the student are not met in the school?

- Continue with a brief discussion to identify preliminary thoughts on needs (sufficient to prepare participants for the upcoming activity but not exhaustive—allow the majority of concepts to emerge through the activity).

ACTIVATION:

- Divide participants into two groups using a ratio of about 1 to 6 (i.e., for each person in Group 1, have 5 or 6 people in Group 2). Give each participant in Group 1 a copy of the whole person from Puzzle Person, and give each participant in Group 2 body parts from Puzzle Person.

- **Group 1** (whole person):
    - Participants move outside the room and discuss amongst themselves needs that students and family members may have. They write 6 different needs on the back of each puzzle person. The puzzle people should be unique—no two lists of needs should be the same! Sample:

Kids are struggling in school

English language help

Food shortage

Need work

Baby has a fever

Feeling helpless, alone, confused

- **Group 2** (body parts):
    - Participants in this group work together or in smaller groups to identify services, both in the school and in the community, that newcomer youth and their parents can access for support. They write one service on each body part.
    - Services should be as specific as possible (e.g., not "food bank," but "North York Harvest Food Bank").
    - Continue until each person has a service written on their pieces.

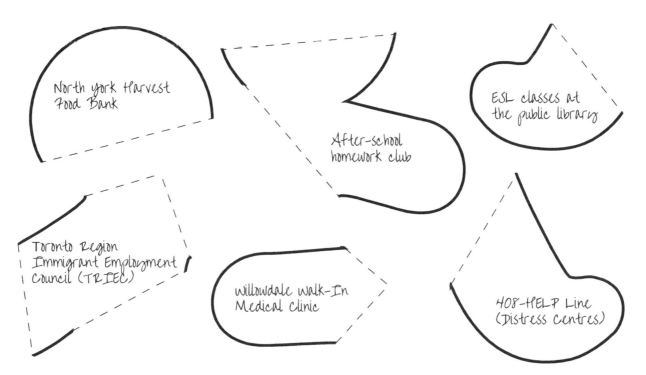

North York Harvest Food Bank

After-school homework club

ESL classes at the public library

Toronto Region Immigrant Employment Council (TRIEC)

Willowdale Walk-In Medical Clinic

408-HELP Line (Distress Centres)

- Disperse members of Group 2 throughout the room and invite members from Group 1 to return to the room. Participants from Group 1 search the room for appropriate resources to meet their needs. They attach body parts to their person until the puzzle is filled or until the resources are all taken. A complete puzzle person will have 6 needs listed on the back and 6 resources attached to the front. (This activity should take 20–30 minutes.)

- Optional variation: Reflect the language barrier that many refugees and newcomers face by not allowing participants to speak during the second part of the activity (the search for services) and by having needs/services written in a different language where possible.

ACQUISITION:

- Once puzzles have been completed as much as possible, bring the group back together to review the needs and services that were brainstormed in the activity.

- On three different pieces of chart paper, list
  - identified needs that "received" services;
  - identified needs that went unmet (were not connected to a service);
  - services that were not utilized.

- Ask: Are there needs or services that are missing?

APPLICATION:

- Lay four pieces of chart paper around the room. Each sheet of chart paper should have one of the following questions written at the top:
  - Why were some needs unmet?
  - Why were some services not used?
  - Were there needs/services that were not identified?
  - How confident are you that you can provide appropriate direction to a student (or family) that requires assistance?

- Divide the group into four small groups, and assign each group to a specific sheet of chart paper.

- Groups have several minutes to think about their question and record thoughts.

- After a few minute, groups move counter-clockwise to the next sheet of paper and spend time thinking about the new question and adding to the notes made by the previous group.

- Repeat until all participants have had an opportunity to go through all of the questions.

- Groups then review all of the information contributed by all groups and share major ideas with the group.

ASSESSMENT:

- Revisit anticipatory questions on the extended role of the teacher and the consequences for students if needs are unmet.

- Exit Slip: Have participants provide feedback on how teachers can ensure the best service is being provided.

PUZZLE PERSON

TEACHER LESSON 26: UNDERSTANDING LOSS AND GRIEF

Objectives	Understand the role of loss and grief in the learning process
Themes	**THEME 7b:** Loss and Grief
Standards and Guidelines Competency Areas	C2.2: Communicate Effectively C2.1: Respect Diversity C2.3: Develop Productive Interactions with Clients
Materials	• List of losses posted or projected where all participants can see it (see below) • *Syria: My Life Before the War* (UNHCR, 2016): https://www.youtube.com/watch?v=7JUcdXQArcs • *Letters to Our Children: The Memories, Challenges & Dreams of Mothers New to Canada.* (Winnipeg, MB: KidBridge Press, 2014): http://www.kidbridge.ca/styled-5/index.html • Pens/pencils • Paper/chart paper • "How to Help Your Students Deal with Grief and Loss" by Kit Richert, Teaching.com: http://teaching.monster.com/benefits/articles/1927-how-to-help-your-students-deal-with-grief-and-loss

Note: This lesson may be emotional for participants who identify with the content of the stories and/or loss. Respect and safety are essential, as well as time to debrief. The lesson is not meant to re-traumatize anyone, but to shed light on the struggles students and their families experience, and to identify supportive strategies. At the end of the lesson, the facilitator can urge any participants who are particularly upset by the activity to seek support for personal losses that remain unresolved.

ANTICIPATORY SET:

- Grief and loss are often thought of in terms of the death of a loved one, which is, of course, extremely significant. Refugee students and their families can experience loss on multiple levels. Place the following list of losses where all participants can see it:
  - Loss of a partner/family/friends
  - Loss of home
  - Loss of independence
  - Loss of safety
  - Loss of culture/community
  - Loss of language
  - Loss of economic stability
  - Loss of identity

- Watch the short UNHCR video *Syria: My Life Before the War*: https://www.youtube.com/watch?v=7JUcdXQArcs

ACTIVATION:

- Identify areas of loss suggested by the video.

- Encourage respectful conversation and sharing around individual experiences of loss (do not be limited by the examples above).

- Distribute stories from Letters to Our Children to participants (you may want to pair participants up as there are 17 stories). Allow participants time to read and to make notes addressing loss reflected in the story.

- Have participants read their stories to the group one at a time. Identify the loss in each story. Allow time for other participants to make connections and share reflections.

- Recognize the sacrifices parents make to give their children opportunities for a safe and successful life.

Note: This book is written by mothers but this is not meant to minimize the sacrifices made by fathers, grandparents, and others. This is noted in the book's acknowledgements as well.

ACQUISITION:

- Discussion questions:
    - Have you considered the process of (forced) migration in terms of loss?
    - Does your program/school/division provide support to students and their families? If so, how?
    - What can we do to support those who have experienced loss within the classroom? Within the school building or educational system?
    - What resources are available?

APPLICATION:

- Have participants write a brief and confidential reflection on an experience of loss (theirs or someone else's).
    - Identify emotions experienced.
    - What helped, what didn't, what might have?

- In table groups, participants generate a list of helpful strategies that could be applied at the classroom level and at the school level for students experiencing loss and grief. Groups share their lists to compile a master list of strategies from which participants may choose those that are useful within their individual workplaces.

- Before participants leave, explain that experiencing this lesson might have been uncomfortable for some participants and elicited intense emotions within them as they reflected on their own personal losses. Some of the brainstormed strategies may be adapted for personal use.

ASSESSMENT:

- Write a brief reaction to the stories and strategies shared during the lesson.
  - Identify emotions experienced.
  - What was most surprising?
  - What challenges seem insurmountable?
  - What strategies seem promising?

TEACHER LESSON 27: TRAUMA

Objectives	Recognize the signs and symptoms of trauma and their effect on the learning process
Themes	**THEME 7:** Trauma Sensitivity, Mental Health Awareness, and Crisis Response
***Standards and Guidelines* Competency Areas**	C2.1: Respect Diversity
Materials	• Chart paper and markers • "The Effects of Trauma on Schools and Learning," National Child Traumatic Stress Network: http://www.nctsn.org/resources/audiences/school-personnel/effects-of-trauma **Note:** Educators who work with traumatized children are at risk of developing secondary traumatic stress. For more information about risk factors, signs, and self-care, visit the website of the Treatment and Services Adaptation Center: https://traumaawareschools.org/secondaryStress.

ANTICIPATORY SET:

- Address the importance of preparing students for content/circumstances that may trigger previously experienced trauma.

- Discuss the implication of word choices.

ACTIVATION:

- Ask: Who is affected by trauma?
  - Common responses are war affected persons, first responders, domestic violence survivors, survivors of fires or accidents.
  - Everyone has faced adversity at one time or another. Others have experienced life-changing events. Most of us have had to use personal coping strategies to work through difficult events. "Trauma" can be a very open and all-encompassing term. Some say dealing with death is a form of trauma. We can say that everyone has experienced some form of trauma (no one is immune).

- Continue the discussion around trauma by using some of the following questions as a guide:
  - What are some traumatic events that may have affected students (of any background) in your community?
  - How have these events been addressed in the community?
  - What are some needs that persons affected by trauma might have?

- How can we address these needs in our classrooms?
- What resources are you aware for students who need support?

ACQUISITION:

- Divide participants into small groups and give each group a piece of chart paper and a marker.

- Ask the following questions and instruct groups to write down their ideas.
  - What constitutes a traumatic event?
  - What impact does a traumatic event have on students overall?
  - What impact does a traumatic event have on preschool students?
  - What impact does a traumatic event have on elementary school students?
  - What impact does a traumatic event have on middle school students?
  - What impact does a traumatic event have on high school students?
  - How does trauma impact a student's ability to learn?

- Review the answers to these questions posted on the website of the National Child Traumatic Stress Network (NCTSN) at http://www.nctsn.org/resources/audiences/school-personnel/effects-of-trauma. Before reviewing the information for each question online, have groups share what they brainstormed. Once all groups have shared, read the information from the website and have a conversation about it.

- Ask and discuss a new question:
  - What impact does a traumatic event have on school staff?

APPLICATION:

- Read the follow story from the NCTSN website ("Three Boys Get Jumped," http://www.nctsnet.org/sites/default/files/html/three_boys_get_jumped.html).

Robert, Ben, and Raul were walking home from high school. A car drove by playing loud music. Ben recognized a gang member in the car who had earlier threatened him. 'Let's get out of here!" he said. Before the boys could get away, the car stopped and four gang members surrounded them. All three boys were beaten. Ben's nose was broken, Robert's front teeth were knocked out, and Raul received a black eye and a fractured rib. In the weeks that followed, each had a very different reaction in school.

Robert became reluctant to attend school. When he went to school, he did not participate in discussions as much as before and was more irritable with his friends and teachers. Previously a conscientious student, Robert began giving excuses for not completing his homework and did poorly on his most recent exam.

Ben seemed to enjoy the notoriety given him from being jumped, and tended to become more aggressive and outspoken with his peers. In class, Ben expanded his role as class clown, now including the teacher in his sarcastic remarks, for which he was repeatedly sent to the office.

Raul showed no obvious signs at school following the experience. He continued in the same manner with his friends and in the classroom. According to Robert, however, each day Raul insisted on taking a different route home from school from the one they took when they were beaten.

- Facilitate a discussion about this story. Some probing questions you can use to prompt discussion:

- Describe what Robert, Ben, and Raul are each going through/feeling after the event.
- How did this event impact their school activities?
- What could make one student more susceptible to distress than another student?
- How might this event impact other students in the class?
- How might this event impact newcomer and refugee students in the class?
- As a teacher, what would you do to support these students?

- Discuss vicarious trauma and post traumatic stress.
    - What are the common signs and symptoms of trauma and stress?
    - As a teacher, what are some challenges and opportunities in addressing the needs of students affected by trauma and stress?
    - Where could you refer students who need support (individuals/organizations/programs)?

ASSESSMENT:

- Participants share one thing that they learned in this session or something they hope to do with the knowledge they have gained in this session.

- Create a brief case study of a traumatic event. Include potential responses and supports appropriate to the context of the case study.

TEACHER LESSON 28: USING LIFE EXPERIENCES TO DIRECT CAREER CHOICES

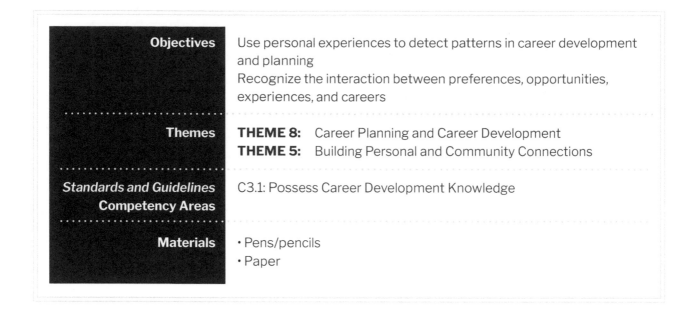

Objectives	Use personal experiences to detect patterns in career development and planning Recognize the interaction between preferences, opportunities, experiences, and careers
Themes	**THEME 8:** Career Planning and Career Development **THEME 5:** Building Personal and Community Connections
Standards and Guidelines **Competency Areas**	C3.1: Possess Career Development Knowledge
Materials	• Pens/pencils • Paper

ANTICIPATORY SET:

- Ask participants to recall when they were in high school. Have them write down the answers to the following questions on a piece of paper:
    - What was your favourite subject? Was it the same as or different from that of your closest friend(s)?
    - What was your favourite activity after and/or before school? Was it the same as or different from that of your closest friend(s)?
    - What would you say was your greatest strength in high school? Greatest challenge?

- Ask:
    - Was it easy to recall high school?
    - What emotions arise thinking about your teenaged years?

ACTIVATION:

- Ask participants to form a line at the centre of the classroom, facing forward. Ask the following questions and have participants step forward if the answer is "yes"; step backward if the answer is "no"; and stand still if the answer is "I don't know/I'm not sure/I can't remember."
    - My favourite subject in high school was also a subject I took in university.
    - My favourite before/after school activity is one I still enjoy today.
    - I am still connected to my closest friend(s) from high school.
    - My current employment allows/requires me to use my greatest strength in high school.
    - My current employment does not allow/require me to use my greatest challenge in high school.
    - Generally speaking, I enjoy my job.

- Ask participants to look at their position in relation to their starting point. Have they taken more steps forward or more steps backward?

- Participants return to their seats. Discussion questions:
  - What were you thinking as you moved forward, stayed still, or moved backward?
  - How is this related to career development and planning?

ACQUISITION:

- In table groups, participants brainstorm a variety of ways in which their current occupation is related to their personality, preferences, life experiences (e.g., Does it require quiet reflection on your own and you are a solitary person? Do you prefer to work with others and your job requires you to collaborate? Is someone you respect and/or love in the same or a related field to you?)

- Share findings as a large group. Allow time for feedback and discussion. Prompts:
  - What patterns do you detect?
  - What types of connections did you see?
  - What were some anomalies? What caused those oddities?
  - What was the most important learning from this activity?
  - How could this activity be adapted for use with students?

APPLICATION:

- As a large group, list careers, occupations, or opportunities that use the same skills as those used by teachers.
  - Circle those jobs that require a university education.
  - Underline those jobs that require advanced training.

- Place an asterisk in front of those jobs that have entry positions open to applicants with a high-school education.

- As a large group, discuss the potential consequences of more and more entry-level jobs requiring a post-secondary education.

- Think about newcomer and refugee students. Consider the following questions for one particular career, e.g., teacher.
  - What obstacles or challenges face newcomer or refugee students in accessing this career?
  - What can schools do to assist newcomer or refugee students in accessing this career?
  - What adjustments, accommodations, or prior learning would be helpful to address these obstacles or challenges?

- Ask participants to think about a variety of other careers and newcomer and refugee students.
  - What careers/occupations come immediately to mind for these students? List them on a piece of paper.
  - Look at your list. Why did you list those careers/occupations?
  - What do your answers to the previous question say about you? (e.g., I self-censor; I restrict opportunities; I consider everything)
  - Brainstorm why many newcomer and refugee students seek entry into professions like medicine, law, and engineering in Canada.
  - Brainstorm activities that would assist newcomer and refugee students to recognize their preferences, skills, and aptitudes and achieve their goals, whatever those might be.

ASSESSMENT:

- Ask each participant to draw a T-chart on a piece of paper. Ask participants to reflect on what they have learned today about themselves and the role of experience and teaching on career development and planning. In the left-hand column, they list of 4 or 5 key learnings. In the right-hand column, they list what they might do in a classroom to assist all students, including refugee and newcomer students, to understand the links between who they are and their working future.

TEACHER LESSON 29: USING MULTIPLE INTELLIGENCES TO INVESTIGATE CAREER OPTIONS

Objectives	Identify strategies to use multiple intelligences to increase career potentials
Themes	**THEME 8:** Career Planning and Career Development **THEME 5:** Building Personal and Community Connections
Standards and Guidelines **Competency Areas**	C3.1: Possess Career Development Knowledge
Materials	• Multiple Intelligences (p. 140) • Pens/pencils • Paper • Mind Map Template (p. 141)

ANTICIPATORY SET:

• Remind participants of the commonly held educational constructs of intelligence quotient (IQ), emotional intelligence (EQ), and multiple intelligences (MI).

• Identifying multiple intelligences in students can not only lead to valuable learning opportunities, but also help determine potential career options. This lesson will look at how professional fields support diversity in interest, skills, and intelligence.

• Remind participants that while young people may demonstrate a higher level of intelligence in one domain over another, they should never be deterred from their passions or limited in their learning as a result. For example, a student struggling in math or science should not be deterred from engineering but could receive support to find a way into the field. Remember too that some students may demonstrate a variety of intelligences.

ACTIVATION:

• Students and educators often hold a somewhat narrow view of professional opportunities. For example, working in agriculture translates into being a farmer; working in medicine means being a doctor or a nurse. Often, little attention is paid to the diversity that exists among career paths. Other roles within professional fields include technicians, marketing and design personnel, engineers, etc.

• Identifying multiple intelligences can help to guide students into potential opportunities not previously considered. This process is critical to decision-making for all students, regardless of family background, academic scores, or grade level.
   • In groups of no more than 4, review the chart of multiple intelligences (p. 140) to re-familiarize participants with the eight intelligences identified in the work of Howard Gardner (2004).

- Discuss in groups how teachers might recognize these intelligences in students.
- Identify intelligences that may be unintentionally ignored in teaching styles and regular classrooms.

ACQUISITION:

- As a large group, brainstorm a variety of fields such as agriculture, medicine, education, politics, etc. Divide the fields (1–2 per group depending on class size) among the smaller groups in the classroom.

- In original small groups, create a mind map of employment opportunities in the assigned field(s) (see the template on page 139). Make note of which intelligences may suit or be drawn to those opportunities; you could have participants group the opportunities by intelligence, as in the following sample mind map:

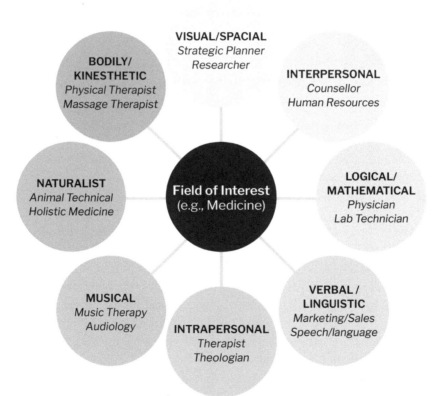

- After an appropriate time (20–30 minutes; allow time for research if necessary), move groups to different tables to review and add to their colleagues' maps. Repeat this group rotation 2 or 3 times.

- Participants return to their original group to review and prepare to present their findings to the class.

- Share findings as a large group. Allow time for feedback and discussion.
    - What types of additions were made to the table group lists by others? (Discuss the role of blind spots in teaching for intelligences that are unlike the teacher's preferred learning style.)
    - What was the most important learning from this activity?
    - How could this activity be adapted for use with students?

APPLICATION:

- Create an eye catching poster to make students aware of the various opportunities available within a field of interest. The poster should be creative enough to foster intrigue while still containing factual information it would be helpful for students to know (specific job titles, education requirements, salary expectations, etc.). Participants may need research their field to learn more about specific opportunities.

Alternative:

- Groups prepare a 1– to 2–page document (or brochure) instead of a poster.

- Groups present their document/brochure to the class and provide an electronic copy to all participants. This way, participants obtain a variety of documents with information on different fields that they can take back to their classrooms and use when talking about career options with youth, as a resource for teachers, or as handouts for students interested in the different fields.

ASSESSMENT:

- Create a T-chart. Ask participants to brainstorm a variety of teaching strategies in the left-hand column. In the right-hand column, list the learning style(s)/intelligence(s) that apply to each teaching strategy.

MULTIPLE INTELLIGENCES

Based on the work of Howard Gardner; see *Frames of Mind* (New York: Basic Books, 2004).

Visual/Spatial
Able to visualize and conceptualize large and/or small spaces
e.g., architect, pilot, interior designer

Interpersonal
Able to interact well with others; empathic
e.g., politician, teacher, human resources professional

Logical/Mathematical
Able to think and problem solve sequentially; understanding of numbers
e.g., accountant, computer programmer, detective

Verbal/Linguistic
Comprehension of word meanings, rhythms, and sounds
e.g., journalist, teacher, comedian

Intrapersonal
Understanding of self, strengths, and capabilities
e.g., artist, counsellor, writer

Musical
Understanding of rhythms, pitch, and tone; able to compose
e.g., songwriter, musician, DJ

Naturalist
Knowledge, appreciation, and understanding of living things
e.g., farmer, resource officer, meteorologist

Bodily/Kinesthetic
Strong body control and coordination; understanding of how parts work
e.g., athlete, physical therapist, mechanic

MIND MAP TEMPLATE

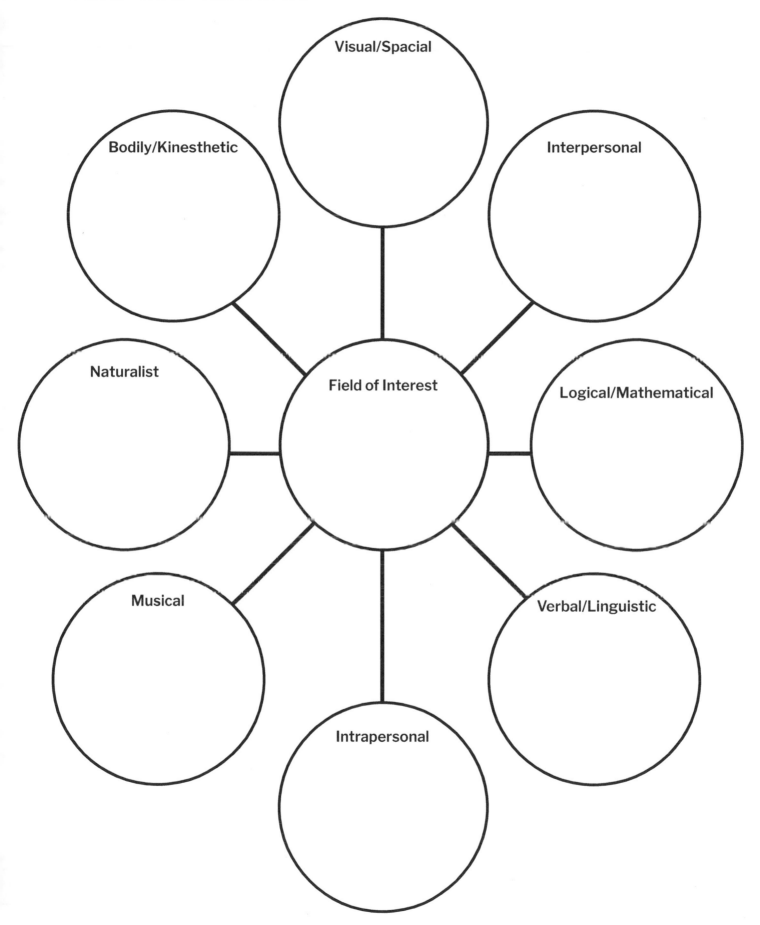

TEACHER LESSON 30: BUILDING SELF-RESILIENCY

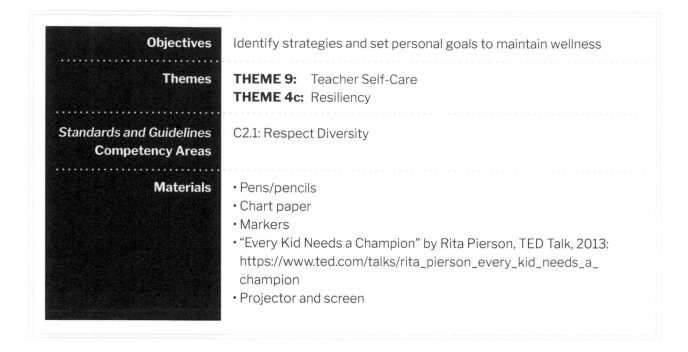

Objectives	Identify strategies and set personal goals to maintain wellness
Themes	**THEME 9:** Teacher Self-Care **THEME 4c:** Resiliency
Standards and Guidelines Competency Areas	C2.1: Respect Diversity
Materials	• Pens/pencils • Chart paper • Markers • "Every Kid Needs a Champion" by Rita Pierson, TED Talk, 2013: https://www.ted.com/talks/rita_pierson_every_kid_needs_a_champion • Projector and screen

This lesson is designed to help educators take care of themselves so that they can be champions for their students. New educators may discover a range of numeracy and literacy skills within their classroom, both below and above grade level. They will also have a variety of social needs that they will have to factor in when considering the health and well-being of every student in every classroom.

ACTIVATION:

Think

- Take 2 minutes to describe a teacher who believes that "every kid needs a champion."
- What do such teachers look like, sound like, act like? What do you believe they know?

Pair

- Take 1 minute to share your answers with person closest to you.

Share

- As a group, describe this person by combining everyone's answers onto a large chart paper.

ACQUISITION:

Watch Rita Pierson's TED Talk: https://www.ted.com/talks/rita_pierson_every_kid_needs_a_champion

Rita Pierson, a teacher for 40 years, once heard a colleague say, "They don't pay me to like the kids." Her response? "Kids don't learn from people they don't like." This is a rousing call to educators to believe in their students and actually connect with them on a real, human, personal level.

Using one participant to take notes on chart paper, ask participants to respond to Rita's response and her talk overall.

APPLICATION:

- If you agree with Rita Pierson that every child needs a champion how can you as a teacher also practice self-care when you have a class full of children with multiple, varying needs?

- If you disagree with Rita Pierson, explain your thoughts with the classroom. How do you feel teachers can practice self-care when they have a class full of children with multiple, varying needs?

- How can you, as the "Rita Pierson" in your classroom, take care of your well-being while still caring for your students? Write actions that you need to do for yourself to not burn out. Place those actions near your daily planner.

- Commit to reading your 5 actions monthly, and addressing at least 1 per week. Begin each month by checking in with yourself to see what needs to be adjusted, added, or altered. Consider sharing how you take care of yourself with your students, to model how they can attend to their needs.

Note: This lesson can be adapted for use with students, particularly at the beginning of a school year or semester. Modelling self-care strategies is viable in every classroom, especially for students in grade 7–12 as they adjust to new routines in school and are learning how to be independent learners.

ASSESSMENT:

- Ask participants to write down some of the things they learned and how these can be applied in different situations. If they feel comfortable doing so, participants can share their ideas with the large group or table group.

SECTION THREE

LEARNING OUTCOMES AND INSTRUCTIONAL IDEAS FOR ALL STUDENTS

• • • • •

Know yourself. Know your audience.

All lessons related to refugee and newcomer experiences require educator mindfulness.

Be aware of unintended consequences, particularly when teaching vulnerable populations.

Be alert for, attuned to, and aware of the signs and symptoms of personal and participant distress.

INTRODUCTION

Student learning outcomes for career development are part of the core curriculum for social studies, health education, language arts, and comprehensive and developmental guidance and counselling programs. They are found in curriculum documents such as Health Education, Career and Life Management, Career Studies, and Life/Work Exploration. These outcomes, or indicators, come from the *Blueprint for Life/Work Designs* (National LifeWork Centre, 2010).

The *Blueprint for Life/Work Designs* was produced by an international partnership, with input from career, curriculum, and human resources specialists across Canada. The *Blueprint* maps out the competencies citizens need to cultivate, from childhood to adulthood, to manage their life/work development (Haché, Redekopp, & Jarvis, 2006). The *Blueprint*'s clear learning outcomes remind educators that all children and youth begin designing their lives during elementary school and become more focused on work-related skills as they move through the school system. For refugee and newcomer children and youth in particular, these learning outcomes become keys to successful futures in their new country.

THE BLUEPRINT FOR LIFE/WORK DESIGNS

To support and engage newcomer and refugee children and youth of all ages, three components require attention: knowledge of self, knowledge of others, and knowledge of the cultural environment. The *Blueprint* touches on all of these, with 11 competencies organized around three areas:

Area	Competency	
Personal Management	1.	Build and Maintain a Positive Self-Image
	2.	Interact Positively and Effectively with Others
	3.	Change and Grow Throughout One's Life
Learning and Work Exploration	4.	Participate in Life-Long Learning Supportive of Life/Work Goals
	5.	Locate and Effectively Use Life/Work Information
	6.	Understand the Relationship Between Work and Society/Economy
Life/Work Building	7.	Secure/Create and Maintain Work
	8.	Make Life/Work Enhancing Decisions
	9.	Maintain Balanced Life and Work Roles
	10.	Understand the Changing Nature of Life/Work Roles
	11.	Understand, Engage In, and Manage One's Own Life/Work Building Process

Each competency is broken down into four levels, to target the developmental stages people go through as they grow. At each level, there are indicators that describe specific knowledge, skills, and attitudes for life-work development. These indicators cover four stages in the learning process: acquisition, application, personalization, actualization.

On the following pages you will find the learning indicators for Levels 1, 2, and 3 of each competency in the *Blueprint*. (Level 4, which targets adult populations, has been omitted.) Suggestions for classroom instruction are provided for each level.

DISCERNING LEVELS OF STUDENT KNOWLEDGE, SKILL, AND UNDERSTANDING

Educators differentiate instruction based on the knowledge, skills, and understanding of their pupils. Thus, the grade levels provided for the activities below serve as guideposts only. We expect educators to use their knowledge of human development, psychology, and pedagogy to select appropriate activities for their students and adapt them as needed to address gaps and support positive growth.

● ● ● ●

SUGGESTIONS FOR INSTRUCTION

COMPETENCY 1
BUILD AND MAINTAIN A POSITIVE SELF-IMAGE

LEVEL 1 (GRADES K–4)

INDICATORS

Acquisition

1.1a1 Understand the concept of personal characteristics such as interests, dislikes, personal qualities, strengths and weaknesses

1.1a2 Discover how positive characteristics are the basis of a positive self-image

1.1a3 Understand how self-image influences behaviours

1.1a4 Understand how personal behaviours influence the feelings and behaviours of others

Application

1.1b1 Identify positive characteristics (skills, interests, personal qualities and strengths) about self as seen by self and others

1.1b2 Demonstrate behaviours and attitudes reflective of a positive self-image

Personalization

1.1c1 Assess one's self-image and evaluate its impact on self and others

Actualization

1.1d1 Transform behaviours and attitudes in order to improve one's self-image

SUGGESTIONS FOR INSTRUCTION

1.1a1 **Self-Inventory.**
Have students perform a self-inventory using sentence primers such as *I am..., I am good at..., I enjoy..., I would like to be better at...*, etc.

1.1a2 **Tic-tac-toe.**
Students create original emoticons or emoji to demonstrate different emotions. (To distinguish game players, have each student use a different colour of paper or otherwise mark their emoti-

cons, e.g., name or initials.) Discuss the feelings associated with the emotions depicted and how different experiences can leave lasting positive or negative feelings about self. Create grids on tables with masking tape and have students play tic-tac-toe with their emoticons or emoji.

1.1a3, 1.1a4   Quilt.

Create a paper quilt with each student contributing a minimum of two squares. (See the template on page 204). First, identify events, activities, and/or behaviours that lead to positive and negative feelings. Discuss how others respond to both positive and negative behaviours. Then, invite students to depict their feelings on their squares. Allow students to use words, drawings, and/or cut-outs. Connect all the squares to make a quilt that illustrates a range of behaviour and emotions and their effects.

1.1b1   About Me I.

Have students list 10 things about themselves—interests, qualities, skills, etc. For example: I play the piano. I speak French. I help my baby brother get dressed. I love bugs. On completion, ask students to identify the best 3 things on the list and place stickers next to those interests/qualities. Have students pair up, and have each student tell 3 best things about their partner. Discuss whether or not these things were on each student's own list, and why or why not that may be.

1.1b1   About Me II.

Have students give 5-minute presentations about themselves to the class. (Alternative: Partners present each other to the class.) Focus on the strengths and qualities discussed in the previous activity.

1.1c1   Attitude.

Have students conduct an experiment: For an entire day, students should smile, say hello, and offer a helping hand (hold a door, help carry something, etc.) to people they interact with. Have students pay attention to how people respond and how they themselves feel as the day goes on. Discuss this experience as a class the following day. Reflect on feelings and make connections to mood, interactions with others, and feelings about self. (Optional: Repeat the experiment with a different attitude: sad, in a bad mood, unhelpful.)

1.1d1   Be the Teacher.

Create opportunities for leadership in the classroom where students can take turns being the "expert" and teaching others about something important to them, such as favourite activities or hobbies, home country, cultural practices, food, etc. Work with students to prepare for their leadership role (e.g., what do they need, would they like to invite someone important to them to help teach their classmates).

COMPETENCY 1
BUILD AND MAINTAIN A POSITIVE SELF-IMAGE

LEVEL 2 (GRADES 5–8)

INDICATORS

Acquisition

1.2a1   Discover how behaviours and attitudes influence the feelings and behaviours of others

1.2a2   Discover how behaviours and attitudes affect school and family situations

1.2a3   Understand how the environment influences attitudes and behaviours

1.2a4   Understand the concepts of values and beliefs, and explore their influence on self-image

1.2a5   Discover the importance of developing realistic and positive self-image, and the consequences of developing an erroneous one

1.2a6   Discover how a realistic and positive self-image contributes to self-fulfillment, both personally and professionally

Application

1.2b1   Describe one's self-image

1.2b2   Adopt behaviours that reflect a positive attitude about self

Personalization

1.2c1   Evaluate the impact of one's self image on self and others

Actualization

1.2d1   Transform behaviours and attitudes in order to improve one's self-image and in turn contribute positively to one's life and work

SUGGESTIONS FOR INSTRUCTION

1.2a1   What is Self-Image?
Have students examine the term *self-image*. What does it mean? Discuss positive and negative self-image.

1.2a2–1.2a6 Self-Image.
Discuss the saying "You are your own worst critic." Ask:
- What does this saying mean?
- Can you think of a time when you've been unfairly hard on yourself for something you said or did?
- How do people develop either a positive or negative self-image?
- Can you think of a time when you were very nervous or down on yourself over something that other people didn't think was a big deal?
- In what ways can negative self-image be damaging to your life?
- How can someone with a negative self-image start to develop a more positive self-image?

1.2b1, 1.2b2 Self-Criticism.

    View the commercial "You're More Beautiful than You Think" by Dove (https://www.youtube.com/watch?v=litXW91UauE). Prompt a discussion about self-criticism that explores more than simple appearances.

1.2c1 What I See, What You See.

    Give students a recipe card and have them write descriptive characteristics of themselves. Have "thought bubble" printouts available (two per student). Break students up into groups and have group members take turns sitting with their back to a wall and a thought bubble taped on the wall to either side of them. Other group members write characteristics to describe the seated student in the thought bubbles. Continue until everyone has had a turn. How do the characteristics in the thought bubbles compare with those on each student's recipe card? Invite students to discuss why they chose the characteristic(s) they did—focus on each person's perspective rather than their observations.

1.2d1 Behind the Mask.

    Distribute blank mask templates (any kind—animal, oval, superhero, etc.). Have students write things about themselves they allow people to see on the outside of the mask. On the inside/back, have them write one or more hidden things that they would like others to see. Prompt discussion about vulnerability, allowing students to lead and discuss among themselves how they might find confidence to share more of themselves in a positive way.

COMPETENCY 1
BUILD AND MAINTAIN A POSITIVE SELF-IMAGE

LEVEL 3 (GRADES 9–12)

INDICATORS

Acquisition

1.3a1 Understand how individual characteristics such as interests, skills, values, beliefs and attitudes contribute in achieving personal, social, educational and professional goals

1.3a2 Understand the importance of giving and receiving feedback

1.3a3 Understand the importance of allies (e.g., relationships, mentors) and external assets (e.g., finances, goods) in the fulfillment of life/work scenarios

Application

1.3b1 Identify the behaviours and attitudes that mirror one's self-image

1.3b2 Identify one's personal characteristics such as interests, skills, values, beliefs and attitudes

1.3b3 Identify one's allies and external assets

1.3b4 Demonstrate giving and receiving feedback

1.3b5 Adopt behaviours and attitudes that project a positive self-image

1.3b6 Adopt behaviours and attitudes conducive to reaching one's personal, social, educational and professional goals

Personalization

1.3c1 Assess one's personal characteristics and capitalize on those that contribute positively to the achievement of one's personal, educational, social and professional goals

Actualization

1.3d1 Improve one's self-image in order to contribute positively to one's life and work

SUGGESTIONS FOR INSTRUCTION

1.3b1 Privilege Simulation.
Facilitate a privilege simulation (see Teacher Lesson 8: Privilege Walk, p. 67).

1.3b2 About Me.
Have students prepare a presentation about themselves in the third person (i.e., do not use I, use name as if speaking about a stranger). They should think about meeting and researching themselves as for the first time. Presentations can be in the form of a video, TED Talk, Prezi, or PowerPoint highlighting personal attributes.

1.3b3 Web.
Using a web template, and with *self* at the centre, ask students to label the different communities/groups/places they interact with (e.g., school, family, soccer team, public library, community

centre). Why do they go there? What do they get from that place/group? Which people are important to them in each of those places/groups? Why?

1.3b4   Minute to Win It.

Partner students up to participate in Minute to Win It challenges. The challenges are quick and fun! One student attempts the challenge while the other observes. When the minute is up, the observer gives the doer suggestions and feedback for doing better. The doer acts on the feedback and attempts the challenge again before students switch roles. (Sample Minute to Win It games from the Canadian Active After School Partnership: http://activeafterschool.ca/activities/minute-win-it-games.)

1.3b5, 1.3b6   Altruistic Project.

Tapping into what students have discovered about themselves in the previous activities, they come up with a small altruistic project to help others that calls on personal strengths, interests, and goals. (Projects for this purpose must be carried out locally and in a short amount of time.) Have students keep a journal to record their plan, process, outcomes, and personal reflections. Discuss how planning and achieving the goals of this project relate to setting and achieving life goals.

1.3c1   Role Play.

Create role-play scenarios that take place in home, school, community, and professional environments. Include opportunities for conflict, creativity, and leadership. Assign roles for students to take on as they work toward desirable outcomes. Students take turns participating and observing, with observers providing constructive feedback to participants. Have participants identify characteristics they called on to achieve the task and others they'd like to improve on in the future.

1.3d1   My Goals.

Have students set small, consistent goals for achievement (social, self-actualizing, and/or academic). For example: I will not participate in gossip for one day; I'm going to find someone who looks like they need a friend and sit with them at lunch this week; I'm going to investigate post-secondary opportunities this month. Student should write the goal in a personal journal and identify at least one personal strength that will help achieve the goal and one area of growth to work on. At the end of the predetermined timeframe, students evaluate themselves. Was the goal achieved? What went well? What could have been done better?

COMPETENCY 2
INTERACT POSITIVELY AND EFFECTIVELY WITH OTHERS

LEVEL 1 (GRADES K–4)

INDICATORS

Acquisition

2.1a1 Discover the unique character of individuals

2.1a2 Explore sources and effects of peer pressure

2.1a3 Explore implications, effects and consequences of helping others.

2.1a4 Explore interpersonal and group communication skills

Application

2.1b1 Demonstrate effective skills, knowledge and attitudes for interacting with others

2.1b2 Demonstrate effective skills, knowledge and attitudes for resolving conflicts with peers and adults

2.1b3 Demonstrate appropriate behaviours and attitudes when peer pressures are contrary to one's beliefs

2.1b4 Demonstrate openness to the diversity of cultures, lifestyles as well as mental and physical abilities

2.1b5 Demonstrate a willingness to help others

2.1b6 Adopt behaviours and attitudes that contribute to positive and effective interactions with others in interpersonal and group settings

Personalization

2.1c1 Acknowledge and appreciate the unique character of one's self

2.1c2 Re-examine one's behaviours and attitudes in interpersonal and group communication contexts and determine those that contribute to positive and effective interactions with others

Actualization

2.1d1 Improve one's interpersonal and group communication skills in order to build positive relationships in one's life

SUGGESTIONS FOR INSTRUCTION

2.1a1 Who Am I?

Have students create riddles about themselves using words and/or drawings. For example: *I like to play soccer. I live with my mom and my brothers. My favourite food is zigni with injera. Who am I?* Put all the riddles in a container and have students take turns choosing and reading a riddle out loud for the class to solve. To help students identify the person each riddle is about, you could have students stand while the riddles are being read, and each time a student is incorrectly identified, that student sits down.

2.1a2 Peer Pressure.

Ask students to identify a time when they did something they didn't want to do. Why did they do it? Where did any pressure come from? Be sure to identify positive as well as negative examples—peer pressure can cause people to take unnecessary risks but can also push people out of their comfort zones to try something new or intimidating. **Note:** Peer pressure can differ greatly according to demographics, maturity, and/or environmental exposure. Find supporting videos and/or books to fit the needs of your classroom.

2.1a3 Helpful or Not?

Part 1: Have students pair up. In a large space (e.g., gymnasium), ask one member of each pair to carry 4–5 large (but light) and awkwardly shaped items a designated distance. Then, have students repeat the task with their partner's help. Discuss how working together made the task more manageable and easier to accomplish.

Part 2: Before you begin, make copies of Square Puzzle (p. 207). Each pair will need an envelope with the puzzle pieces cut out and a copy of the solution. A copy of the blank template for the puzzle (see p. 208) is optional but recommended.

Assign A and B designations to the pairs. Meet with the Bs separately to explain the activity: Their partners (the As) are going to start solving a puzzle, but when you give an agreed-upon signal, the Bs will take over and finish it. Give the Bs a copy of the solution to study, so that they can solve the puzzle easily. Tell them to be sure they don't show the solution to their partners!

Give the As an envelope with the cut-out puzzle pieces and ask them to assemble the pieces into a square. After 2 minutes or so, give the signal for the Bs to take over.

Discuss: How did the As feel about their partners' help? Was it appreciated? What happens when we don't have the opportunity to solve a problem on our own? Compare and contrast the two kinds of helping illustrated in these activates. (Worth noting that good intentions may not always be helpful!)

2.1a4 Follow Instructions.

Have students pair up, and give each pair two small sets of identical wood blocks, dice, or dominoes (5 pieces for each partner). Assign number 1s and number 2s. Pairs should spread out and sit back-to-back so that partners cannot see each other's work.

Number 1s create a structure, and number 2s tries to replicate the structure based only on the verbal instructions of their partner, e.g., *Place two blocks side by side standing tall and another on its flat side across the top.*

Allow 3 or 4 minutes for partners to work, then have partners reveal their structures to each other. Are they the same? If not, how are they different? Was there confusion in the communication? What would have been helpful?

Alternative option: Have students face each other at a table with a physical barrier between them. Number 1s build their structure behind the barrier, and then communicate instructions using only hand gestures.

2.1b1–2.1b6 Teamwork.

Divide the class into groups of no more than 5. Have each group work together to complete a timed challenge such as the Marble Track Instant Challenge found at https://www.homeschool-creations.net/marble-track-instant-challenge-logic-for-kids/. (There is no need to keep score as the focus is on effective communication and teamwork.)

Once the challenge is complete, debrief with the following discussion questions:
- What went well?
- Were everybody's ideas acknowledged? Did anyone have an idea and not say anything? Why?
- What could you have done differently to make your group work more effectively?

Following this discussion, ask group members to discuss their challenge and offer feedback to each other. Repeat the activity and debrief once again to determine what changed in how the group worked together and if they were more successful in meeting the challenge.

2.1c1. Coat of Arms.
Have student draw or use cut-out images to create a coat of arms that reflects who they are and what is most important to them. If you provide students with a template, it can be divided into labelled sections—such as family, talents, goals, favourite things—or left blank for students to determine how these elements fit.

2.1c2 Television Ad.
Select appropriate and relevant samples of television ads from the Pass It On series here: http://www.values.com/inspirational-stories-tv-spots. Have students work in groups to create their own Pass It On television ads reflecting their own interaction in the school or greater community. Ads can be recorded or acted out.

2.1d1 Conversation Cafés.
Students are grouped at tables and given a topic at random to talk about. The goal is to practice the communication skills of active listening, responding, and inquiry. For example, if table 1 has the topic My Weekend, individuals take turns talking about their weekend. Listeners provide their undivided attention and listen without interrupting, while asking for further information (e.g., Which park did you go to?) and offering responses that affirm they are listening.

Offer time at the end of the café for self-reflection with questions such as the following:

- Did you feel your group listened to you? Why or why not?
- What behaviours did you appreciate (or not)?
- Where you attentive to your group members? Did you listen with interest? Where you distracted?
- Are there things you would like to improve on next time?

Participation in regular cafés throughout the year will build relationships and communication skills.

COMPETENCY 2
INTERACT POSITIVELY AND EFFECTIVELY WITH OTHERS

LEVEL 2 (GRADES 5–8)

INDICATORS

Acquisition

2.2a1 Explore the concept of diversity as it relates to respect, tolerance, flexibility and openness towards others

2.2a2 Explore the concepts of dependability and honesty towards others

2.2a3 Explore interpersonal and group communication skills

2.2a4 Explore personal management skills such as time management, problem solving, stress management, life-work balance, etc.

2.2a5 Explore helping skills such as facilitating, problem solving, tutoring and guiding

Application

2.2b1 Demonstrate respect for the feelings and beliefs of others

2.2b2 Demonstrate tolerance and flexibility in interpersonal and group situations

2.2b3 Demonstrate skills, knowledge and attitudes in responding to criticism

2.2b4 Demonstrate effective social and group membership skills, knowledge and attitudes

2.2b5 Demonstrate openness to the diversity of cultures, lifestyles, as well as mental and physical abilities

2.2b6 Demonstrate helping skills such as problem solving, tutoring and guiding

2.2b7 Demonstrate dependability and honesty towards others

2.2b8 Demonstrate personal management skills such as time management, problem solving, stress management, life-work balance, etc.

Personalization

2.2c1 Acknowledge and appreciate the similarities and differences among people

2.2c2 Re-examine one's respect, tolerance, flexibility, openness, dependability and honesty towards others and determine to what degree they are influencing the development of positive relationships in one's life

2.2c3 Integrate personal management skills such as time management, problem solving, stress management and life/work balance to one's daily life.

2.2d1 Engage in further learning experiences that help build positive relationships in one's life

3

SUGGESTIONS FOR INSTRUCTION

2.2a1 **Four-fold Profile.**

Fold a sheet of paper in half, and then fold it in half again so it is divided into four parts. In one part, have students draw the flag that identifies their home country or the country that they identify with most closely. (Canadian-born students may identify with Canada or a country that reflects their ancestry.) In another part, students write the name of the country and a typical greeting. In a third part, they share one thing that they are proud of and that might make them different from others; and in the last part, they write or draw something that makes them the same as other people. Have everyone share. Guide discussion around respect towards differences.

2.2a1 **What Colour is Your World?**

Consider what different colours mean in different cultures and to different individuals. Invite students to share associations and uses of colours they know about in their own culture(s), and share with them information about other cultures. (One possible article to share with students: "What Colors Mean in Other Cultures," by Smarter Travel, *The Huffington Post*, January 26, 2016, http://www.huffingtonpost.com/smartertravel/what-colors-mean-in-other_b_9078674.html). Read the book *My Many Coloured Days* by Dr. Seuss (New York: Random House, 1996) to help get students thinking about personal relationships and reactions to colour. Have students create a one-colour picture or a demonstration of what a colour means to them personally or what significance it has to their family or culture.

2.2c1, 2.2c2 **Garden of Differences.**

Our similarities can make us compatible; our differences make us beautiful. Create a garden of differences by cutting flower petals out of patterned and coloured paper. On the back of each petal, have students write something that they feel makes them different or unique. Once several petals have been written on, start to assemble flowers on a designated board or as a border around the room. Discuss how all these differences come together to create something lovely and unique.

COMPETENCY 2
INTERACT POSITIVELY AND EFFECTIVELY WITH OTHERS

LEVEL 3 (GRADES 9–12)

INDICATORS

Acquisition

2.3a1   Discover the skills, knowledge and attitudes needed to work effectively with and for others

2.3a2   Explore helping skills such as problem solving, tutoring and guiding

2.3a3   Examine appropriate employee–employer interactions and client–contractor interactions in specific situations

2.3a4   Explore personal management skills such as time management, problem solving, personal financial management, stress management, life-work balance, etc.

Application

2.3b1   Demonstrate behaviours and attitudes required for working with and for others

2.3b2   Demonstrate personal management skills such as time management, problem solving, personal finances, stress management, life/work balance, etc.

2.3b3   Express feelings, reactions and ideas in an appropriate manner

2.3b4   Demonstrate helping skills such as problem solving, tutoring and guiding

Personalization

2.3c1   Determine the helping skills one feels comfortable with and wishes to contribute in relationships with others

2.3c2   Acknowledge the positive effects of expressing one's feelings, reactions and ideas

2.3c3   Integrate personal management skills such as time management, problem solving, stress management and life/work balance to one's life and work

Actualization

2.3d1   Engage in further learning experiences that help build positive relationships in one's life and work

SUGGESTIONS FOR INSTRUCTION

2.3a1   **How Will You Improve?**

Draw a T-chart, and list on one side the skills, knowledge, and attitudes needed to work *with* others. On the other side, list skills needed to work *for* others.

Have students bring in 5 different job ads from the newspaper or an online source. Ask them to identify the skills, knowledge, and attitudes they think will be needed for these jobs and add any to the T-chart that are not already listed.

Have students conduct a personal assessment using the ideas generated above. Have them rate themselves on each item: 1—needs work, 2—doing okay, or 3—mastered.

Students now develop a plan for improving personal skills. Ask: What needs to improve? How will you improve? Make a list of three goals to work on over the next 3 months to improve personal skills.

2.3a3 Sticky Situations.

Develop scenarios featuring difficult employee–employer or client–contractor interactions. For example: *You are a customer who needs flooring for a new home. The contractor and a representative from the flooring company come to your house with samples. You pick a sample, pay a deposit, and order the flooring. When the flooring arrives, it is the wrong colour and does not match the existing room. The flooring company insists this is the closest colour. You think the colour is not close and doesn't work. What would you, as the homeowner, do? What do you think the contractor should do? What can be done to resolve this problem?*

Write up possible scenarios and put them in a hat. Have students choose scenarios and generate positive and mutually agreeable solutions. Students can role-play scenarios with their resolutions.

2.3b4 Teaching and Learning.

Have student pick something they feel confident doing—a skill or task they feel they could teach or guide someone else to do. Examples include administering CPR, tuning skis, sewing clothing, painting a picture, knitting a hat, or fixing a flat bike tire. Encourage students to pick a unique skill that might be difficult or complicated for others to learn.

Have students break down the skill or task into as many separate steps as possible, put the steps on index cards, and then see if someone else can perform the skill or task by following the index cards, without any direct coaching or guidance from the student.

Next, have each student share the steps with a learner using photographs, drawings, or videos. Note any differences to the learning using each process.

Finally, have each student work one-on-one with a person to help them learn the skill or complete the task.

COMPETENCY 3
CHANGE AND GROW THROUGHOUT ONE'S LIFE

LEVEL 1 (GRADES K–4)

INDICATORS

Acquisition

3.1a1   Explore the concepts of change and growth as part of life

3.1a2   Understand that change and growth impact on one's mental and physical health (e.g., stress, frustration, confusion, fatigue)

3.1a3   Explore personal feelings (mental and physical)

3.1a4   Explore ways to express feelings

3.1a5   Explore good health habits

3.1a6   Explore the importance of asking for help and ways to do so

Application

3.1b1   Express feelings

3.1b2   Demonstrate good health habits

3.1b3   Ask for help when needed

Personalization

3.1c1   Acknowledge the positive effects of expressing one's feelings

3.1c2   Acknowledge the positive outcomes of asking for help

3.1c3   Re-examine one's health habits and adopt those that contribute positively to one's growth

Actualization

3.1d1   Engage in good health habits

SUGGESTIONS FOR INSTRUCTION

3.1a1   Now I Can...
Ask students to think about things they are able to do now that they could not do by themselves before (e.g., tying shoelaces, crossing the street, making breakfast, riding a bike, going to the mall with friends). Discuss some of the characteristics involved in growing and gaining independence, and what kind of responsibilities are included. Examine how those characteristics continue to develop into adulthood and how responsibilities change.

3.1a3, 3.1a4   Feelings Charades.
Write feelings on index cards (e.g., happy, sad, angry, frustrated, bored), and distribute the cards to the class. Each student draws a face that expresses the feeling on their card(s). Collect the completed cards and play a game of Feelings Charades. One at a time, students pull a card from the pile and act out the feeling. (Allow students who are at a loss to ask for help if necessary.)

Classmates guess the feeling. Once the feeling has been correctly identified or revealed, briefly discuss why the student chose to demonstrate the way they did, what physical actions can be associated with the feeling (e.g., smiling or laughing with happy), as well as possible causes.

3.1a6, 3.1b3   Help!

Have each student think of one thing they would like, or need, help with at school (e.g., reading, math, friends, sport). One by one, students can reveal their "help" request. Students who are willing and/or able stand up and reveal how they can help (e.g., I can help with that! I'll show you how to..., I can read with you..., I can go with you...). Follow-up discussion should help students understand that by working together and asking for help they can achieve their goals.

3.1b2   Healthy Habits.

Have students identify healthy habits they practice for their body, brain, and heart. You can record these in the template on page 207 using words and/or drawings.

3.1b3   Friendship Bracelets.

Create friendship bracelets using string and pony beads. Collect beads in as many colours as possible (minimum 10) and distribute them to students (one colour per student). Offer examples of a time help was needed or help was given to someone else. Discuss the qualities (characteristics) that the helper showed in those examples (e.g., kind, encouraging, thoughtful) and write them on the board. As a group, assign a different "helper" characteristic to each bead colour. Ask students to choose 5 of the characteristics they think are the most important and to create a bracelet pattern using the corresponding colours. Students can use coloured pencils and either blank paper or a template to record patterns. Students then share patterns with the group, explaining why they chose the colours (characteristics) they did and why these are important to them. To create their bracelets, students must ask others for the required beads. Practice different ways of asking for beads, e.g., Are you able to help me with my bracelet? Can you give me a bead please? Place a limit on how many beads each student can give away if multiple students have the same colour. Optional: As an opportunity to practice generosity, students may give their completed bracelet away.

3.1c3, 3.1d1   My Health Journal.

Create booklets for students to keep track of their behaviour, habits, choices, and interactions with others. (See the template on page 208. Students complete entries on the page throughout the week, reflecting on experiences and setting goals for the week to follow.)

COMPETENCY 3
CHANGE AND GROW THROUGHOUT ONE'S LIFE

LEVEL 2 (GRADES 5–8)

INDICATORS

Acquisition

3.2a1   Explore how feelings are influenced by significant experiences

3.2a2   Understand the concept of stress and its impact on mental and physical well-being

3.2a3   Explore effective communication skills to use in stressful situations (assertiveness, conflict resolution, problem solving, etc.)

3.2a4   Discover changes that occur in the physical, psychological, social and emotional development of an individual

3.2a5   Understand how physiological and psychological changes impact on life and work

3.2a6   Explore the importance of work, family and leisure activities to mental, emotional, physical and economic well-being

Application

3.2b1   Identify what causes stress on one's own mental and physical being

3.2b2   Demonstrate effective communication skills in stressful situations (assertiveness, conflict resolution, problem solving, etc.)

3.2b3   Identify one's own physical, psychological, social and emotional changes

Personalization

3.2c1   Re-examine one's communication skills and adopt those that are truly effective in stressful situations

3.2c2   Examine one's work, family and leisure activities and acknowledge their impact on one's mental, emotional, physical and economic well-being

Actualization

3.2d1   Improve communication skills used in stressful situations

3.2d2   Engage in further work, family and leisure activities that contribute to one's mental, emotional, physical and economic well-being

SUGGESTIONS FOR INSTRUCTION

3.2a1, 3.2a2, 3.2b1   **Responses to Stress.**

It is difficult to avoid stress; we all experience some amount of it. Stress is a response that the body has when a demand is made upon it. Stress is unique to every person and each person copes with it in their own way.

Have students make a list of the different events or experiences which might cause them to feel stress (e.g., worrying about an upcoming test, making new friends). Now, on a scale of 1 (lowest) to 10 (highest), have them indicate their personal level of stress in each situation. For the three situations that cause the most stress, ask students to list feelings or behaviours they experience in each situation. Sample feelings and behaviours include headaches, sweating, skin rash, tense muscles, grinding or clenching teeth, nail biting, hair twisting, aggressiveness, irritability, sadness, no energy, difficulty sleeping.

On the outline of a person, have students draw or write how they personally experience stress. They can use any of the feelings and behaviours listed previously. On a second outline, have student list the opposite: how they feel and behave when they are not stressed.

Have students put their two outlines side by side on a larger piece of paper. Between the outlines, invite students to show what a person could do to alleviate stress. Examples might include exercising, eating properly, talking to a trusted friend, gaining a new skill, managing time, being with friends.

Have students keep a journal or use an electronic notes application to keep track of what upsets them or causes them stress and also what calms them or helps to relieve stress.

3.2b2 Patience Principles.

Discuss the principles of effective communication: negotiation, compromise, mediation, conflict resolution, assertiveness. Teach students the Patience Principles (Stewart, 2002) to help them remember tips on handling themselves assertively.

P - Pick a good time and place to talk.
A - Avoid using general words like *never* and *always*, e.g., "You always interrupt me."
T - Talk about only one issue at a time.
I - "I messages" work best, e.g., "I feel hurt that you forgot to call me."
E - Eliminate exaggeration and criticism.
N - No put-downs or insults.
C - Clarify what you meant to say and what you heard the other person say.
E - Examine and explore other possible points of view and different opinions.

(*The Anger Workout Book for Teens* by Jan Stewart, San Bernardino, CA: Jalmar Press, 2002, p. 60)

Write up some sample scenarios and practice using the Patience Principles to discuss something contentious or solve a problem.

COMPETENCY 3
CHANGE AND GROW THROUGHOUT ONE'S LIFE

LEVEL 3 (GRADES 9–12)

INDICATORS

Acquisition

3.3a1   Describe how change and personal growth affect physical and mental health

3.3a2   Explore how mental and physical health impact on life/work decisions

3.3a3   Explore stress management strategies

Application

3.3b1   Demonstrate behaviours and attitudes that maintain physical and mental health

3.3b2   Apply stress management strategies

Personalization

3.3c1   Examine one's mental and physical health and evaluate its impact on life/work decisions

3.3c2   Acknowledge the positive outcomes of applying management strategies to one's life and work

Actualization

3.3d1   Adopt habits and engage in experiences that maintain or improve one's mental and physical health

3.3d2   Improve one's life and work management strategies

SUGGESTIONS FOR INSTRUCTION

3.3a3   Stress Management.
Generate a list of possible stress management strategies, and develop a personal "toolbox of techniques" to help decrease stress. Examples might include go for a walk, hang out with a friend, do yoga, do mindfulness activities, play with a pet, exercise, go out in nature, read a book, listen to music. Students can put each suggestion on a piece of paper and gather the papers in a box/ jar, or they can create a list in a journal. They should commit to picking and practising one of the activities in their toolbox each day.

Have students find apps and websites that are helpful for reducing stress (e.g., mindfulness, meditation, anxiety-reduction). Conduct an in-class rating of any apps or websites students are already using or are interested in using.

COMPETENCY 4
PARTICIPATE IN LIFE-LONG LEARNING SUPPORTIVE OF LIFE/WORK GOALS

LEVEL 1 (GRADES K–4)

INDICATORS

Acquisition

4.1a1 Understand the importance of preparing for one's life and work paths

4.1a2 Explore how skills, knowledge and attitudes acquired in school can be useful at home, in the workplace and in the community

4.1a3 Explore subject area strengths as well as areas to improve

4.1a4 Explore strategies for improving academic skills and knowledge

4.1a5 Discover how different levels of work require different combinations of acquired skills, knowledge and attitudes

4.1a6 Explore multiple work types and alternatives, both paid and unpaid

4.1a7 Explore the relationship between ability, effort and achievement

4.1a8 Understand the importance of practice, effort and learning

Application

4.1b1 Demonstrate effective information-gathering strategies

4.1b2 Apply strategies for improving academic skills and knowledge

Personalization

4.1c1 Evaluate one's strategies for gathering information or improving academic skills and knowledge and adopt those that contribute best to one's learning process

Actualization

4.1d1 Improve learning strategies

SUGGESTIONS FOR INSTRUCTION

4.1a1–4.1a8   Future Me.

Students create a picture book, PowerPoint, or Prezi presentation about themselves now or in the future, using any one or more of the following prompts/sentence starters:

Me Today
- What I'm learning today for tomorrow
- Things I'm good at
- Things I want to improve and how I will improve
- When I grow up, I think I want to be _____ because...
- This is what I do to help out in my community

Me in the Future
- This is where I work
- This is how I got here
- These are the skills I developed
- This is what I do to help out in my community

4.1a6, 4.1b1   Jobs/Roles in the Community.

Take a walk around the community and have students look for and identify jobs at various business and services. Back in the classroom, let students choose one of the jobs or roles they think they might be interested in and prepare a short oral presentation about the job/role and how it contributes to the community. Use books, the internet, and people as sources for research.

4.1b2, 4.1c1, 4.1d1   Learning Styles.

Students participate in a research experiment on their own learning. They begin by choosing a topic of interest (animal, sport, person, etc.). Students then gather information on their topic from three different types of sources: text (e.g., books, newspaper articles, blog posts); video (e.g., films, how-to videos); and people (e.g., interviews, storytelling). Each source reflects a different learning style: linguistic, visual, auditory. Students should reflect on what and how they learned from each type or source. Ask: Which type of source/learning styles did you prefer? Why? What did you learn from this that can help your learning in the future?

COMPETENCY 4
PARTICIPATE IN LIFE-LONG LEARNING SUPPORTIVE OF LIFE/WORK GOALS

LEVEL 2 (GRADES 5–8)

INDICTORS

Acquisition

4.2a1 Explore life-long learning strategies

4.2a2 Explore subject area strengths as well as areas to improve

4.2a3 Explore strategies for improving academic skills and knowledge

4.2a4 Understand how personal skills and attitudes influence life and work-related successes

4.2a5 Understand the relationship between personal beliefs, attitudes and skills, and life and work choices

4.2a6 Explore the importance of both the academic and practical skills in the workplace

4.2a7 Explore the skills, knowledge and attitudes needed in specific work sectors

4.2a8 Explore the skills, knowledge and attitudes best suited to adapt to changing work role requirements

4.2a9 Understand how current academic performance may impact the selection of high school programs/courses

4.2a10 Understand how current academic performance may impact work

Application

4.2b1 Demonstrate life-long learning strategies

4.2b2 Apply strategies for improving academic skills and knowledge

4.2b3 Demonstrate personal skills and attitudes conducive to life and work successes

4.2b4 Compare how one's own role as a student is similar to that of a worker's role

Personalization

4.2c1 Evaluate one's strategies for improving academic skills and knowledge and adopt those that contribute best to the learning process

4.2c2 Evaluate the impact of one's personal skills and attitudes to one's life/work successes

Actualization

4.2d1 Improve and engage in life-long learning strategies supportive of one's life/work scenarios

SUGGESTIONS FOR INSTRUCTION

4.2a1–4.2a10   Personal Inventory.

Have students complete the following inventory:

1. Who are you? Write as many details about yourself as possible. Create a "personal story" that best describes who you are.
2. What do you do with your time? What do you like to do? What are you committed to doing? What do you need or have to do?
3. Where do you live and go to school? Where do you want to live? Where do you want to travel or visit in the future?
4. When do you enjoy doing activities? When is your most productive time of the day? How do you choose what to do each day?
5. Why do you do the things you do? Why do you study? If you have a job, why do you work? If you volunteer, why do you volunteer?
6. How do you spend your time and money?
7. How do you solve problems or get along with others?

Using the answers above, have students choose three different jobs or work sectors that interest them. Run through the Who, What, Where, When, Why and How questions and have students answer them for the chosen jobs.

Ask students to consider how their personal skills and attitudes and who they are as people are conducive to life/work success.

COMPETENCY 4
PARTICIPATE IN LIFE-LONG LEARNING SUPPORTIVE OF LIFE/WORK GOALS

LEVEL 3 (GRADES 9–12)

INDICATORS

Acquisition

4.3a1   Understand how academic and work skills, knowledge and attitudes contribute to achieving personal goals

4.3a2   Understand how skills, knowledge and attitudes acquired in academic and technical/practical programs may contribute to achieving personal and professional goals

4.3a3   Understand how life-long learning enhances the ability to achieve goals

4.3a4   Understand how education relates to the selection of post-secondary programs, workplace training and/or entry into work

4.3a5   Understand how a set of skills, knowledge and attitudes can fulfill the requirements of a variety of work roles and work environments

4.3a6   Understand why life-long learning is required in the workplace

4.3a7   Explore various work role requirements

Application

4.3b1   Demonstrate life-long learning behaviours and attitudes that contribute to achieving personal and professional goals

4.3b2   Demonstrate how one's education relates to various options regarding post-secondary programs, workplace training and/or entry into work

Personalization

4.3c1   Determine the value of continued learning for oneself

4.3c2   Determine one's transferable skills, knowledge and attitudes that can fulfill the requirements of a variety of work roles and work environments

Actualization

4.3d1   Engage in a continuous learning process supportive of one's life/work goals

SUGGESTIONS FOR INSTRUCTION

4.3a1–4.3a5   Career Information.
Attend a career symposium or trade fair. Have students choose 3–5 career options to focus on as they collect information and interview representatives. Each student should prepare in advance an index card with interview questions such as the following:

- What are some of the things I would do in this job?
- What are some of the skills required to do the job well?

- How can I obtain these skills? What kind of training/education is required?
- What do employers in the field expect from employees?

Optional extension: Students can interview someone working in each career field they explored. Potential interview questions include: Why did you choose this career? How did you prepare? What skills did you have/acquire? What do you like most/least about your career? What are some of the things you do?

4.3a6 Timeline.

Ask students to select a professional field and create a timeline of how it has evolved over the last 100 years. Identify trends, technological advancements, and social/environmental impacts and responsibilities.

4.3a7 Fields and Industries.

Work together to identify and display different roles and positions in the Education field. Begin with positions at the school level, which students will be familiar with (e.g., teacher, guidance counsellor, principal, education assistant). You may introduce positions from other levels too (e.g., board superintendent, Minister of Education). Have students work independently (individually or in small groups) to do the same for another field, industry, or workplace (e.g., automotive industry, library).

4.3b1 Personal and Professional Goals.

Ask students to declare one personal and one professional goal. How are their current behaviours helping or hindering them in achieving those goals? What can they do or change to help make these goals a reality? Students can use the graphic organizer on page 209 to organize their answers.

4.3c1, 4.3c2 Career Opportunities.

Many online tools use an algorithmic database to assist students in exploring career opportunities based on identified strengths, talents, and knowledge. Explore sites available in your province and those licensed by your school district to find useful tools for activity planning in the classroom. Examples:

- Career Cruising—https://public.careercruising.com/en/
- Set Your Course Manitoba—http://www.setyourcourse.ca/
- Manitoba Career Prospects—http://manitobacareerprospects.ca/

COMPETENCY 5
LOCATE AND EFFECTIVELY USE LIFE/WORK INFORMATION

LEVEL 1 (GRADES K–4)

INDICATORS

Acquisition

5.1a1 Explore work of family members, school personnel and community workers/employers

5.1a2 Explore work roles and settings of interest to oneself

5.1a3 Explore the concept of work information and how parents, relatives, adult friends and neighbours can provide this information

5.1a4 Discover how interests, knowledge, skills, beliefs and attitudes relate to work roles

5.1a5 Explore various working conditions of work roles (e.g., inside/outside, hazardous)

5.1a6 Understand how self-employment differs from working for others

5.1a7 Explore various sources of work information (e.g., networks, internet, television, newspapers)

Application

5.1b1 Use various sources of work information (e.g., internet, television, newspapers)

Personalization

5.1c1 Express one's opinion on work information that one has explored

Actualization

5.1d1 Improve one's strategies for locating and using work information

SUGGESTIONS FOR INSTRUCTION

5.1a1 Job Board.

Brainstorm as a class a list of jobs people around you have. Create a bulletin board or wall display of photos or drawings of as many people as can be collected, and include a small write-up that identifies the person, what their job is, and what they do in that job. Include professions family members may have had in a previous country.

5.1a2–5.1a5, 5.1c1 Career Day.

Designate a day or afternoon for students to come dressed as someone in a chosen profession. In preparation, students will research the profession by talking to adults in the community, including family members, and examining other available resources (books, videos, etc.) to learn more about day-to-day life in that profession. On Career Day, students will introduce themselves. For example: "My name is Mohammed and I am a real estate agent. I knew I wanted to do this because… School/training required was… I work in an office and out in the community. My favourite part of my work is… I think this is a good career choice for me because…"

You could also invite family/community members to Career Day to share their professional experience and expertise.

5.1a6 Who's the Boss?

Revisit the bulletin board or wall display from **Job Board** (see above). Who are the administrators/supervisors for each of the employees pictured? What does it mean to have a supervisor/boss? What does it mean to work for yourself? What might be some of the challenges in working for yourself or others?

5.1a7, 5.1b1 Sources of Information.

As part of **Career Day** research (see above), have students search for employment ads or training opportunities for their chosen career. Use printed resources such as local newspapers; online sources such as Indeed (http://www.indeed.ca) or Service Canada (https://www.canada.ca/en/services/jobs.html); as well as community bulletin boards, local television stations, and people in the community.

5.1a7, 5.1b1 Scavenger Hunt.

Create a scavenger hunt that requires students to find information related to employment opportunities, training, and roles of workers. Sample items:

- Find an advertisement for a job that requires a university degree
- Find an advertisement for a massage therapist
- Find a school that offers training for electricians

Students can provide clippings, web addresses, and/or photographs for each item.

COMPETENCY 5
LOCATE AND EFFECTIVELY USE LIFE/WORK INFORMATION

LEVEL 2 (GRADES 5–8)

INDICATORS

Acquisition

5.2a1   Discover differences between work, jobs, occupations and careers

5.2a2   Discover how occupations, work roles and work alternatives (e.g., self-employment, contracting, multi-tracking) can be classified

5.2a3   Explore economic/work sectors

5.2a4   Explore school and community information resources on work roles and work alternatives

5.2a5   Discover how skills, knowledge and attitudes can be transferable from one work role to another

5.2a6   Explore various work settings and work roles in the community

5.2a7   Explore various working conditions (e.g., inside/outside, hazardous)

Application

5.2b1   Use school and community settings and resources to learn about work roles and work alternatives

5.2b2   Demonstrate how one's interests, knowledge, skills, beliefs and attitudes are transferable to various work roles

5.2b3   Identify working conditions for oneself

Personalization

5.2c1   Assess life/work information and determine its pertinence for oneself

Actualization

5.2d1   Improve one's strategies for locating, understanding and using life/work information

SUGGESTIONS FOR INSTRUCTION

5.2a4, 5.2a5   Job Jot Notes.

Have students visit a community resource centre or have someone from the centre come to talk to the class about different jobs in different fields. Have students make jot notes about the jobs, and also the knowledge and attitudes necessary in each work role. Students then pair up to pool their notes and develop a list of skills needed for various jobs.

Rules for making jot notes:
- Record keywords and themes so they make sense to you later.
- Use bullet points.
- Don't use full sentences.
- Don't worry about punctuation.
- Start each new idea on a new line.

5.2a7 Workplace Health and Safety.

Have someone come to speak to the students about workplace health and safety. Have them make jot notes about the various potential hazards in different workplaces. Discuss what students could do if they were asked to perform a hazardous task as part of employment. What could they say or do? Who could they talk to? Have students write up possible scenarios and then role-play how they might act in each situation. Sample scenarios:

- You are working in a fast food restaurant and you are asked to climb up to the top of a fryer to clean the grease.
- You are working as a lifeguard at a beach and there is forked lightening. Your supervisor tells you to take the boat out on the lake to pull in some buoys.

5.2b2 Transferable Skills.

Discuss the concept of transferable skills and create a list of such skills. Have students consider a variety of occupations and the skills that are needed for each. (Use a list of occupations such as this one from the Government of Canada: https://www.jobbank.gc.ca/jobsearch/ jobsearch?sort=M&searchstring=occupations&button.submit=Search) As you read out occupations in different categories, ask students to put a tick next the transferable skills on their list that might be required in that occupation. Once you have read out about 20 different occupations, have students tally the ticks. Discuss the skills, knowledge, and attitudes that are required across many, if not most, occupations.

COMPETENCY 5
LOCATE AND EFFECTIVELY USE LIFE/WORK INFORMATION

LEVEL 3 (GRADES 9–12)

INDICATORS

Acquisition

5.3a1 Explore the educational and training requirements of various work roles

5.3a2 Discover how key personnel in selected work roles could become ideal information resources and/or role models

5.3a3 Explore how trends and work opportunities in various economic/work sectors impact the nature and structure of work roles

5.3a4 Explore how employment and workplace trends impact education and training scenarios

5.3a5 Understand how a variety of factors (e.g., supply and demand for workers, demographic changes, environmental conditions, geographic location) impact work opportunities

5.3a6 Understand how labour market information (profiles, statistics, etc.) should be used when making life and work decisions

5.3a7 Explore a variety of work alternatives (e.g., full employment, multi-tracking, contracting, consulting, entrepreneurship)

Application

5.3b1 Use career information resources such as career monographs, occupation classification systems, labour market information, mass media, computer and internet based career information delivery systems to educate oneself to the realities and requirements of various work roles

5.3b2 Consult key personnel in selected work roles as information resources, role models and/or mentors

Personalization

5.3c1 Determine, according to one's preferences, the advantages and disadvantages of various work alternatives (e.g., full employment, multi-tracking, contracting, consulting, entrepreneurship)

5.3c2 Assess life/work information and evaluate its impact on one's life/work decisions

Actualization

5.3d1 Improve one's strategies to locate, interpret, evaluate and use life/work information

SUGGESTIONS FOR INSTRUCTION

5.3a3–5.3a7 Write a Business Proposal.
> Ask students to consider a business they would be interested in establishing. Have them search for a template to follow and write a proposal for the business. In their proposal, they should justify the need for the business, describe how it would contribute to the community, estimate overhead

costs and the time it would take to turn a profit, and identify potential employment opportunities for others. Students should also consider these questions:

- Are there other businesses and services (e.g., contractors, banks) that could help your business get off the ground. What would these services cost? Are there free or less costly alternatives available through government or cooperative groups?
- Who are your competitors and how will you compete?
- Will your business operate year-round or only during certain seasons?

Students should present their business plans to the class and allow for critical questions from classmates that require a "defence." After each presentation, the class can vote on whether or not the business seems feasible.

COMPETENCY 6
UNDERSTAND THE RELATIONSHIP BETWEEN WORK AND SOCIETY/ECONOMY

LEVEL 1 (GRADES K–4)

INDICATORS

Acquisition

6.1a1   Understand how work can satisfy personal needs

6.1a2   Understand how work can contribute positively to society

6.1a3   Explore the products and services of local employers

6.1a4   Explore the impact of work on personal, social, economic and environmental problems

Application

6.1b1   Demonstrate how work can satisfy one's personal needs

6.1b2   Demonstrate how work might solve personal, social, economic and environmental problems

Personalization

6.1c1   Determine the value of work for oneself

Actualization

6.1d1   Engage in work experiences that satisfy one's needs as well as contribute to one's community (e.g., family, school)

SUGGESTIONS FOR INSTRUCTION

6.1a1–6.1b2   Guest Speakers.

On a bulletin board or other designated wall space, post a map of the surrounding community. Have students help identify businesses and services available throughout the area. Invite speakers from as many of the businesses/service providers as possible to come in and speak to the class about their work and place of employment. Prior to the presentation, have each student prepare and write a question. Guide students to formulate questions about what the work entails, how it contributes to the community, what product or service is provided, what each person likes/dislikes about their job, and what kind of training they needed to do their job. After each presentation, students will ask their questions and record the answers.

Assign student hosts for each of the guests. The host meets the guest at the door, welcomes them, and introduces them to the class. At the end of the presentation, the host thanks the guest for coming and escorts them to the exit. Afterwards, the host collects all of the questions and answers and creates a summary for that business/service to be added to the community map.

COMPETENCY 6
UNDERSTAND THE RELATIONSHIP BETWEEN WORK AND SOCIETY/ECONOMY

LEVEL 2 (GRADES 5–8)

INDICATORS

Acquisition

6.2a1   Understand how organizations operate (e.g., how money is made, overhead costs, profit)

6.2a2   Explore the importance of work to a community

6.2a3   Understand the relationships between work, community and the economy

6.2a4   Explore the economic contributions workers make to a community

6.2a5   Understand how the community, the economy and technological advances impact work and work roles

Application

6.2.6   Demonstrate how work actually impacts one's community

Personalization

6.2.7   Evaluate how one can contribute to the community (e.g., family, school) through work

Actualization

6.2.8   Engage in work experiences that contribute to one's community (e.g., family, school)

6.2a1–6.2a4   Contributing to My Community.

How can we be a constructive and contributing part of our community? Discuss as a class a need within the school or community that can be achieved within the school year or term (repair project, new piece of playground equipment, park bench, etc.). Choose a goal to achieve within a designated time frame.

Establish a fundraising project to raise necessary funds to achieve the goal. Create a framework that includes a timeline, how much needs to be raised, potential partners, overhead costs, preparation, time investment, team roles, and potential outcomes. Note any organizations, businesses, and/or workers that you consult or work with for your project. In what other ways do they contribute to your community?

Throughout the duration of the project, debrief and evaluate progress and effectiveness. Build on ideas that are working and change those that may not be working. Conduct a final evaluation, discussing what you've learned about your community, what your project will mean to the community, and the ability we each have to influence our communities and the people around us.

COMPETENCY 6
UNDERSTAND THE RELATIONSHIP BETWEEN WORK AND SOCIETY/ECONOMY

LEVEL 3 (GRADES 9–12)

3

INDICATORS

Acquisition

6.3a1   Explore the effect of work on people's lifestyles

6.3a2   Understand how society's needs and functions affect supply of goods and services

6.3a3   Explore how trends (such as social, demographic, technological, occupational and industrial trends) can positively and negatively affect work and learning opportunities

6.3a4   Understand the concept of global economy and explore how it affects individuals, communities, the provinces or territories as well as the country itself

Application

6.3b1   Demonstrate how one's community is affected by society's needs and functions, as well as by the global economy

6.3b2   Demonstrate how work and learning in one's community is affected by certain trends (such as social, demographic, technological, occupational and industrial trends)

Personalization

6.3c1   Evaluate the impact of society's needs and functions, and that of the global economy on self

6.3c2   Evaluate the impact of social, demographic, technological, occupational and industrial trends on work and learning opportunities for oneself

6.3c3   Determine the importance of work for oneself

Actualization

6.3d1   Engage in work experiences that satisfy one's needs as well as contribute to society

SUGGESTIONS FOR INSTRUCTION

6.3a1–6.3a4   Poverty, Inc.

View the documentary *Poverty, Inc.* (2014; www.povertyinc.org/education). Compare and contrast employment availability and shortages and the effect of opportunity versus poverty. Have students participate in a debate for and against Western perspectives of "helping." Points of discussion should include empowerment strategies for communities and the importance of work versus charity for social development.

6.3d1   Service Learning.

Have students each find a service learning opportunity in the community (e.g., soup kitchen, hospital, resource centre, community club) and make arrangements to volunteer for a designated period of time. Students should keep a journal of the experience and write entries for each day/time they volunteer. Notes can include a summary of the day's activities, skills developed, interesting people met (e.g., other volunteers, employees of the organization, clients), and any significant moments or experiences. Designate time for discussion in class where students can share their experiences with one another. They can reflect on how each organization contributes to society, and how volunteers and volunteerism in general contribute to society.

Note: Students who work, have heavier academic loads, or have extensive family commitments may have less time to devote to this and can arrange to volunteer less, e.g., once a week for a month. The experience should not be a source of stress but an opportunity to gain self-fulfillment through service to others.

COMPETENCY 7
SECURE/CREATE AND MAINTAIN WORK

LEVEL 1 (GRADES K–4)

INDICATORS

Acquisition

7.1a1   Understand the importance that personal qualities (e.g., dependability, promptness, getting along with others) have on creating, getting and keeping work

7.1a2   Explore creative ways of performing work activities

7.1a3   Understand how cooperation among workers can help accomplish a task

7.1a4   Understand the importance of being able to work with people who are different from oneself (e.g., race, age, gender, people with disabilities)

7.1a5   Understand the meaning of taking responsibility for one's actions

Application

7.1b1   Demonstrate creative ways of performing work activities (e.g., at home, at school, in the community)

7.1b2   Demonstrate the ability to work with people who are different from oneself (e.g., race, age, gender, people with disabilities)

7.1b3   Experience cooperation in order to accomplish a task

7.1b4   Demonstrate the ability to take responsibility for one's actions

Personalization

7.1c1   Re-examine one's experience while performing work activities and determine for oneself which abilities and attitudes contributed positively or negatively to the experience

Actualization

7.1d1   Improve one's abilities and attitudes in order to contribute positively to work experiences (e.g., at home, at school, in the community)

SUGGESTIONS FOR INSTRUCTION

7.1a1–7.1a5, 7.1b1–7.1b4   Team of Superheroes.

Have students create a superhero T-shirt identifying their best quality as their "superpower" (see template on page 210). Ask students to tell how this quality is important to their environment and what it brings to a team. Have students combine their superpowers to create dynamic teams that are able to work together to complete tasks. Students can come up with fun team names that represent all the important qualities.

Write specific tasks on index cards. (Include a wide range of tasks, some challenging and some less so.) Have teams choose a card and determine how they would use their collective super-powers to complete the task. Identify possible personal or group limitations. How might these be overcome? Are there other teams that have something to offer?

7.1c1 **Modified Snakes and Ladders.**

Modify an existing Snakes and Ladders game. The last square, or win, should represent a significant life goal. Each ladder represents a positive attitude or achievement necessary to achieve the goal, and each chute represents a potential setback or frustration. As a class, or in small groups, have students identify the life goal as well as positive and negative events on the journey to the goal; students can use sticky notes to add these to the game board. Students then take turns playing each other's games (or the class game).

7.1d1 **Tower of Success.**

Have each student create a tower of success by writing in each building block on the Tower of Success template (p. 213) a factor, characteristic, or attitude representing how they participate in each of the given areas of life. Create one tower together, to model the process. Begin by talking about how your personal attitude contributes to your self (Me)—to who you are. Show how that attitude contributes to who you are and what you do at home (Me at home), then at school (Me at school), and so on.

COMPETENCY 7
SECURE/CREATE AND MAINTAIN WORK

LEVEL 2 (GRADES 5–8)

INDICATORS

Acquisition

7.2a1   Explore personal qualities (e.g., dependability, punctuality, getting along with others) that are needed to get and keep work

7.2a2   Understand how academic and practical skills are transferable in a variety of work alternatives

7.2a3   Understand the language describing employment and other work opportunities and conditions

7.2a4   Explore work search tools and skills required to find/create and maintain work (job application forms, résumés, portfolios, job interviewing, proposals, cover letters, etc.)

Application

7.2b1   Demonstrate personal qualities (e.g., dependability, punctuality, getting along with others) that are needed to get and keep work

7.2b2   Demonstrate the ability to complete application forms

7.2b3   Develop work search tools required to find and maintain work (e.g., résumé, portfolio, proposals, cover letters)

7.2b4   Identify one's transferable academic and practical skills and experience a new task by using them

Personalization

7.2c1   Acknowledge one's personal qualities and academic/practical skills and determine which to build into one's life/work scenarios

Actualization

7.2d1   Create and engage in new work experiences (e.g., at home, at school, in the community) that acknowledge one's personal qualities and use one's transferable skills

SUGGESTIONS FOR INSTRUCTION

7.2a1, 7.2a2   Complementary Qualities.
Print qualities on sheets of paper and post then around the room with coloured tags or stickers (a different colour per quality). Have students collect the tags/stickers for 2–3 of their most identifiable qualities. As students stand in a circle with everyone's tags/stickers visible, offer examples of school and work tasks. Have students express how their qualities would help them complete the task and identify those in the group with qualities that might complement theirs, so that together they could complete the task better/more quickly.

7.2a3–7.2a4, 7.2b1–7.2b3   Job Applications.
Create a list of websites that have employment postings in your area (e.g., https://www.indeed.ca/, https://localjobshop.ca/). Have students search for listings that interest them. From those listings,

have students pull out requirements and assets and list them vertically on notepaper. In a second column, students explain each requirement or asset using definitions and synonyms.

Students choose one listing and create a cover letter and résumé as though they were applying to the job. If the listing includes a link to a downloadable application form, students can print the form and fill it out. Otherwise, provide or have students search for a template or online builder.

Optional: Students can take turns participating in mock interviews. You could invite community business owners to the class to discuss what employers are looking for and what kinds of questions they ask potential candidates.

7.2d1 Monthly Goals.

Each month, students commit to a goal, e.g., join a group/club at school (or create a new one!), participate in home life in a new way (added responsibility), or volunteer in the community (with a neighbour, business, or organization). At the end of the month, each student gives a brief presentation explaining what they did, what skills they used/developed, what they liked/disliked about the experience, and what their goal is for the next month. Student goals should cycle through home, school, and community.

COMPETENCY 7
SECURE/CREATE AND MAINTAIN WORK

LEVEL 3 (GRADES 9–12)

INDICATORS

Acquisition

7.3a1   Explore skills, knowledge and attitudes required to locate, interpret and use information about work opportunities

7.3a2   Explore skills, knowledge and attitudes that are transferable from one work role to another

7.3a3   Explore work search tools and skills required to seek, obtain/create and maintain work (job application forms, résumés, portfolios, job interviewing, proposals, cover letters, etc.)

7.3a4   Explore specific work opportunities in terms of working conditions, benefits, etc.

7.3a5   Explore employability or workability skills, knowledge and attitudes necessary to obtain and maintain work (e.g., adaptability skills, information about the organization, risk-taking attitude)

7.3a6   Explore services or initiatives that support the transition from high school to work or further education/training

7.3a7   Understand that work opportunities often require flexibility and adaptability (e.g., relocating, learning new skills)

7.3a8   Explore volunteering as a proactive job search and personal development strategy

Application

7.3b1   Demonstrate the skills, knowledge and attitudes in preparing personal marketing documentation (e.g., résumés, proposals, portfolios, cover letters)

7.3b2   Demonstrate the skills, knowledge and attitudes necessary for a successful work interview

7.3b3   Demonstrate employability skills, knowledge and attitudes necessary to obtain and maintain work

7.3b4   Experience volunteering as a proactive job search or personal development strategy

Personalization

7.3c1   Evaluate work opportunities in terms of working conditions, benefits, etc., that are important to oneself

7.3c2   Acknowledge one's personal set of skills, knowledge and attitudes that contribute to seek, obtain/create and maintain work

Actualization

7.3d1   Create and engage in work opportunities reflective of one's personal set of skills, knowledge and attitudes

7.3d2   Adapt or innovate one's work search skills and tools

SUGGESTIONS FOR INSTRUCTION

7.3a3   Sources.

Ask students to explore sources of employment opportunities, including websites (general, industry-specific, or organization-specific), newspapers, and community bulletins. Brainstorm findings as a group. Assign individuals to each of the previous sources. Have them prepare presentations addressing the kind of employment opportunities found in each, as well as the advantages and limitations of each. Determine which sources are preferable for a variety of searches (e.g., part-time, full-time, temporary, career, volunteer).

Create a job board in the classroom where updated employment opportunities can be posted. Groups of students can take turns monitoring, updating, and adding opportunities from a variety of sources.

7.3b1, 7.3b3   Personal Website.

Using a free developer (e.g., Weebly, Wix), students can create a personal website designed to market themselves. Paying attention to style and design, the website should offer information that includes skills, talents, goals, and interests. The website should read like an electronic portfolio and include notable achievements and samples of relevant pieces of work. Students can develop a polished résumé to post as a downloadable option.

7.3b2   Mock Interviews.

Establish a script for students to use in mock employment interviews. Discuss do's and don'ts to consider when being interviewed. Pairs will take turns being the interviewer and the interviewee. After the interview, have the interviewer provide constructive feedback, including positive responses and behaviours as well as things to work on for future interviews.

COMPETENCY 8
MAKE LIFE/WORK ENHANCING DECISIONS

LEVEL 1 (GRADES K–4)

INDICATORS

Acquisition

8.1a1   Understand how choices are made

8.1a2   Explore what can be learned from experiences

8.1a3   Explore what might interfere with attaining goals

8.1a4   Explore strategies used in solving problems

8.1a5   Explore alternatives in decision-making situations

8.1a6   Understand how personal beliefs and attitudes influence decision-making

8.1a7   Understand how decisions affect self and others

Application

8.1b1   Assess what might interfere with attaining one's goals

8.1b2   Apply problem-solving strategies

8.1b3   Make decisions and take responsibility for them

Personalization

8.1c1   Examine one's problem-solving strategies and evaluate their impact on the attainment of one's goals

8.1c2   Evaluate the impact of personal decisions on self and on others

Actualization

8.1d1   Engage in a responsible decision-making process

SUGGESTIONS FOR INSTRUCTION

8.1a1–8.1a3   Decisions, Decisions.

Ask students to guess how many decisions they make each day, week, and month. Brainstorm all the possible decisions they might make in one day (e.g., what to wear, who to play with, what to do at recess) and compile a list. Come up with an estimate of the number of decisions made per week and month. Ask students to consider how they make so many decisions, sometimes at the same time. How do they decide what to do first? Divide the class into groups of 4. Ask each group to come up with a situation where a student has 5–6 different decisions to make. Groups swap situations and decide which decisions to prioritize. They are to write down what they feel the most important decision/problem is and why.

8.1a4 Detective Glass.

Acting like a detective can help us to understand problems before we try to solve them. Distribute copies of the magnifying glass on page 212. Review the questions written on the glass with students.

- **What** happened?
- **Who** is involved?
- **When** did it happen?
- **Where** did it happen?
- **Why** did it happen?

Use the questions to discuss a typical classroom problem/situation — current, past, or imagined. For example:

Two students (Rashpal and Bryan) are arguing at recess. Rashpal told Bryan that he no longer wanted him to come to his party. Rashpal told three other students not to talk to Bryan and now Bryan is alone and upset.

Direct students to focus on answering the questions—and perhaps to ask more questions— before they explore any possible solutions.

8.1b1–8.1b3, 8.1c1–8.1c2   Decision-making in a Group.

Divide students into groups of 4 or 5. Give each group a package of straws and masking tape. Explain that each group must design the tallest freestanding structure they can using only these two materials. Each group should appoint one observer to take notes about how the process develops and how decisions are made. After groups have had time to make the structure, hold a large-group discussion.

- How were decisions made? What process did each group use to create their structure?
- What happened when things were not going well? How did group members solve any problems that occurred?

Have students consider the impact of their personal decisions on others. Did anything surprise them about themselves or others?

COMPETENCY 8
MAKE LIFE/WORK ENHANCING DECISIONS

LEVEL 2 (GRADES 5–8)

INDICATORS

Acquisition

8.2a1 Understand how personal beliefs and attitudes affect decision-making

8.2a2 Understand how career development is a continuous process with a series of choices

8.2a3 Explore possible outcomes of decisions

8.2a4 Explore school courses related to personal, educational and work interests

8.2a5 Understand how the expectations of others affect career building

8.2a6 Explore ways in which decisions about education and work relate to other major life decisions

8.2a7 Explore advantages and disadvantages of various secondary and post-secondary programs for the attainment of career goals

8.2a8 Explore the requirements for secondary and post-secondary programs

8.2a9 Understand how uncertainties about the future may lead to creative or alternative choices

Application

8.2b1 Demonstrate how one's beliefs and attitudes influence one's decision-making process

8.2b2 Demonstrate how one's series of choices reflect one's career path

8.2b3 Compare advantages and disadvantages of various secondary and post-secondary programs for the attainment of career goals

8.2b4 Make decisions and take responsibility for them

8.2b5 Develop creative or alternative choices reflective of the changing world of work

Personalization

8.2c1 Evaluate how one's decisions (about school, family, leisure, work, etc.) impact one's life, and affect other decisions

8.2c2 Examine creative or alternative scenarios, and evaluate their impact on one's life

8.2c3 Evaluate the impact of personal decisions on self and on others

Actualization

8.2d1 Engage in decision-making respectful of oneself and supportive of one's goals

SUGGESTIONS FOR INSTRUCTION

8.2a2 Have students keep a list of the activities they do at home. What activities do they contribute to? Do they have a hobby they enjoy or a skill they can do? Activities might include baking, installing Wi-Fi networks, helping care for sick pets, planning meals, refinishing furniture, growing a garden, helping siblings with homework, decorating cakes, interior decorating, changing the oil in cars, changing tires, fixing bikes, repairing appliances, and more. Next to each activity, have students list related careers. Pairs can review each other's lists to see if any other career links could be added.

Now have students consider extracurricular activities they have taken part in. For each activity they have been involved in, now or in the past, they can jot skills they gained. For example:

Activity	Skills I Gained
Violin lessons	Concentration
	Discipline to practice
	Memorization
	Time management
	How to fix an instrument

8.2a4   Make Connections.

Assign students to groups of 4. Have each group take one academic course (e.g., Mathematics, English, Science) and brainstorm some potential personal, educational, and work interests that flow from it. Have groups swap and add to each other's lists. Alternatively, do the opposite: have students identify academic courses related to various interests.

8.2a4, 8.2a8   Post-Secondary Programs.

Explore the entrance requirements for different post-secondary programs. Gather a variety of post-secondary calendars and have students list requirements for various programs. For example: What are the entrance requirements for first-year Engineering, Education, Business, or Fine Arts at university? What are the requirements for a first-year culinary or design program at college? Have students compare and contrast the requirements for different programs. What subjects are needed most often? What is the average grade for acceptance? How do you get scholarships/bursaries? These activities introduce students to the process of applying for different programs and demonstrate how courses in secondary school contribute to a career path. Ensure students explore requirements for various institutions and programs (e.g., hairdressing schools, business schools, universities, colleges).

COMPETENCY 8

MAKE LIFE/WORK ENHANCING DECISIONS

LEVEL 3 (GRADES 9–12)

INDICATORS

Acquisition

8.3a1 Understand the importance of developing a range of scenarios supportive of one's preferred future

8.3a2 Investigate the requirements needed to quality for desired post-secondary education/training

8.3a3 Investigate costs (living and school-related) associated with post-secondary education and training

8.3a4 Investigate strategies for securing financial assistance related to post-secondary education and training

8.3a5 Explore high school courses in terms of skills, knowledge and attitudes required for entry level work or advanced training

8.3a6 Understand the steps required for transition (school to post-secondary education/training programs or work)

8.3a7 Understand how personal values may influence one's choices and actions

8.3a8 Explore how being positive about the future and its uncertainties may lead to creative and interesting possibilities/alternatives

Application

8.3b1 Demonstrate responsibility for making educational and work choices

8.3b2 Develop a range of scenarios supportive of one's preferred future

8.3b3 Plan strategies for covering costs (living and school-related) associated with post-secondary education/training scenarios and apply for needed assistance

8.3b4 Plan and complete the steps required for transition (school to post-secondary education/training programs or work)

8.3b5 Develop creative or alternative choices reflective of the changing world of work

Personalization

8.3c1 Evaluate educational and work choices in terms of one's personal goals, values and financial means

8.3c2 Examine scenarios and alternatives in given decision-making situations and determine if they are supportive of one's values and goals

8.3d1 Create and engage in life/work scenarios supportive of one's values and goals

8.3d2 Engage in decision-making respectful of oneself and supportive of one's goals

SUGGESTIONS FOR INSTRUCTION

8.3a1–8.3a8   Post-School Survival Guides.

Have students prepare questions (at least 10) and interview first-year college/university students or recent high-school graduates who have chosen to enter the workforce full-time. Include questions that explore what each person thought life would be like after high school compared to what it is actually like.

Use all of the findings from the interviews to develop comprehensive survival guides for high-school graduates. Divide the class into two groups. Group 1 will work on the post-secondary guide, and group 2 the employment guide. Assign different topics to individuals or pairs in each group.

Sample Group 1 Topics:

- Being Away from Home for the First Time (financial management, household hints and tips, safety, etc.)
- Study Skills (time management, notetaking, essay writing, text/exam styles, etc.)
- Relationships (healthy relationships, dating violence, the many versions of NO!)
- First-Year Survival for Parents

Sample Group 2 Topics:

- Being Away from Home for the First Time (financial management, household hints and tips, safety, etc.)
- What to Expect in the Workplace (employee/employer relationships, communication, working collaboratively, etc.)
- Getting Along with Others (meeting conduct, problem solving, etc.)
- Relationships (healthy relationships, dating violence, the many versions of NO!)
- First-Year Survival for Parents

Once all components have been researched, you could develop a template (for consistency) and have students enter all research/information into the template.

COMPETENCY 9
MAINTAIN BALANCED LIFE AND WORK ROLES

LEVEL 1 (GRADES K–4)

INDICATORS

Acquisition
9.1a1 Explore the various roles an individual may have (e.g., friend, student, worker, family member)

9.1a2 Explore work-related activities in the home, community and school

9.1a3 Understand how family members depend on one another, work together and share responsibilities

9.1a4 Understand how work roles complement family roles

Application
9.1b1 Experience work-related activities in the home, community and school

9.1b2 Demonstrate how one works with other family members and shares family responsibilities

9.1b3 Demonstrate the links between one's work roles and some of one's family roles

Personalization
9.1c1 Examine one's different life roles and evaluate one's responsibilities within each of them

Actualization
9.1d1 Engage responsibly in each of one's chosen life roles

SUGGESTIONS FOR INSTRUCTION
9.1a2–9.1a4 Preparing for the Future.
How do going to school and doing chores prepare young people for the future? How do these activities contribute to the functioning of family and readiness for adulthood? Brainstorm characteristics of adulthood and write them on the board (leave space between them). Have students start to connect current activities and responsibilities (e.g., making breakfast, getting to school on time, completing assignments) to each characteristic and write these around the characteristics in a different colour. Next, in a third colour, draw bridges/lines between concepts to illustrate how all of these characteristics and activities work together to prepare students for their futures!

9.1b1–9.1b3 Life Swap.
Students can trade roles with a parent or caregiver for a day. Families should choose a day that has few extracurricular and out-of-house activities (community or school programming) and reverse the roles of caregiver and child. If reversing roles in the home is not an option, children can trade roles with someone within the school community for the duration of a school day. Have students share their experience including responsibilities, energy/work required, and anything they learned about their caregiver's role that was new or unexpected.

COMPETENCY 9
MAINTAIN BALANCED LIFE AND WORK ROLES

LEVEL 2 (GRADES 5–8)

INDICATORS

Acquisition

9.2a1 Understand how different work and family roles require varying kinds and amounts of energy, participation, motivation and abilities

9.2a2 Understand how work roles satisfy personal and family needs

9.2a3 Examine how personal goals can be satisfied through a combination of work, community, social and family roles

9.2a4 Understand how personal leisure choices relate to lifestyle

9.2a5 Understand how various life and work roles impact the attainment of future goals

9.2a6 Explore advantages and disadvantages of various life role scenarios

9.2a7 Explore the interrelationships among family, work and leisure decisions

Application

9.2b1 Plan and experience leisure activities that relate to one's considered or preferred lifestyle

9.2b2 Demonstrate how one's various life and work roles impact the attainment of one's future goals

Personalization

9.2c1 Examine the type of lifestyle one wants

9.2c2 Determine the type of life and work roles that would best impact one's life

Actualization

9.2d1 Engage in scenarios that are supportive of one's life/work goals

SUGGESTIONS FOR INSTRUCTION

9.2a1–9.2a2 Daily Log.
Students keep a log of the daily activities of all household members for 2 days. At the end of the 2 days, students create a table that summarizes each activity (prepared breakfast, went to work, attended school, etc.), its purpose, and its impact on the maintenance of the household. Identify any activities that work toward a particular goal (personal or household). Students can summarize how the members of the household work together to create a functioning unit.

COMPETENCY 9
MAINTAIN BALANCED LIFE AND WORK ROLES

LEVEL 3 (GRADES 9–12)

INDICATORS

Acquisition

9.3a1   Understand the concept of life stages and the meaning of each of them

9.3a2   Understand the factors that influence or impact lifestyles (e.g., socioeconomic status, culture, values, work choices, work habits)

9.3a3   Examine how different work scenarios can affect life scenarios

9.3a4   Explore the contribution of work to a balanced and productive life

9.3a5   Understand the importance and impact of leisure activities in one's life

9.3a6   Discover how work skills, knowledge and attitudes can be acquired through leisure and volunteer work

Application

9.3b1   Plan and experience work scenarios reflective of one's life stage and lifestyle

9.3b2   Plan and experience leisure activities that contribute to a balanced life

9.3b3   Demonstrate how work skills, knowledge and attitudes are acquired through one's leisure

Personalization

9.3c1   Examine one's work scenarios and determine which ones are supportive of one's life/work goals

9.3c2   Examine one's leisure activities and determine which ones contribute to a balanced life

9.3c3   Acknowledge the factors that influence or impact one's lifestyle (e.g., socioeconomic status, culture, values, work choices, work habits)

Actualization

9.3d1   Engage in work scenarios and leisure activities that support one's goals and contribute to a balanced life at this stage in one's life.

SUGGESTIONS FOR INSTRUCTION

9.3a1–9.3a2   Snapshots.

Students create an album of photographs from their future life. They can start with a current "selfie" (an actual photograph or a drawing) and continue with self-portraits for each decade up to age 60. Students can draw their self-portraits or use aging software, if available, to age a current photograph. Students should write a short text for each image that describes their possible or desired state at that age (e.g., family status, work, where they live, what they do for entertainment, future goals).

COMPETENCY 10
UNDERSTAND THE CHANGING NATURE OF LIFE/WORK ROLES

LEVEL 1 (GRADES K–4)

INDICATORS

Acquisition

10.1a1 Understand the positive impact of work on people (e.g., higher self-esteem, financial autonomy)

10.1a2 Discover the changing life roles of men and women in work and family settings (e.g., men at home, women in high administrative functions)

10.1a3 Understand how contributions of individuals both inside and outside the home are important to family and community (e.g., family financial autonomy, community volunteering)

Application

10.1b1 Outline the life roles of males and females in one's own family setting

10.1b2 Plan and make contributions both inside and outside the home

Personalization

10.1c1 Examine the type of life roles one would be ready to consider

10.1c2 Examine and acknowledge the positive impact work has on oneself

Actualization

10.1d1 Engage in fulfilling work and life role experiences

SUGGESTIONS FOR INSTRUCTION

10.1a3 Inside and Outside the Home.
Have students make a list of roles people can have both inside and outside the home. Include both paid and unpaid/volunteer contributions. Consider how these roles contribute to the overall family unit.

Distribute copies of the outline of a house on page 213, and have students draw or write the roles/jobs their family members take on inside the home. Next, have students draw stick figures to illustrate the roles of their family members outside the home. Discuss the many roles that people in families may have and the importance of all contributions.

Note: Some students will have same-sex parents or guardians; some students may be living in multi-generational households and/or with members of their extended family; some students, particularly refugee children and youth, may have been separated from close family members. Be mindful of the various situations your students may be in. The purpose of the lesson is to discuss the variety of roles and not to focus on any particular configuration, or a gender that might historically be associated with a role.

10.1a3, 10.1c1 My Roles.

Have students work with a partner to make an outline of their body on a large piece of paper. Ask students to write or illustrate the roles they have (e.g., dog walker, dish washer, swimmer, bike rider, child, grandchild) inside the body. Outside of the body, have students draw large thought bubbles. In each bubble, students use words and/or pictures to illustrate some of the life roles they might want to assume in the future.

3

COMPETENCY 10
UNDERSTAND THE CHANGING NATURE OF LIFE/WORK ROLES

LEVEL 2 (GRADES 5–8)

INDICATORS

Acquisition

10.2a1 Identify non-traditional life/work scenarios

10.2a2 Investigate advantages and challenges of entering non-traditional work

10.2a3 Explore the advantages of experiencing personal interests, even if they are most often considered non-traditional to one's gender

10.2a4 Understand the concepts of stereotypes, biases and discriminatory behaviours

Application

10.2b1 Experience personal interests, even if they are most often considered non-traditional to one's gender

10.2b2 Identify stereotypes, biases and discriminatory behaviours that may limit opportunities for women and men in certain work roles

Personalization

10.2c1 Acknowledge one's own stereotypes, biases and discriminatory behaviours that may limit opportunities for oneself or others in certain work roles

Actualization

10.2d1 Develop attitudes and engage in behaviours that are non-discriminatory

SUGGESTIONS FOR INSTRUCTION

10.2b2 Timeline.
Draw a timeline around the room and have students list historically significant events related to under-represented groups. For example: women being allowed to vote, legalization of same-sex marriage. Ask students to guess what might come next on the timeline (in the future).

10.2c1 Stereotypes.
Put up 7 pieces of chart paper with one of the following labels on each: Jocks, Brains, Hipsters, Gamers, Nerds/Geeks, Artsys, Slackers. (**Note:** Adjust this list of labels as needed to suit your school, students, and area.) Have students walk around the room and write what comes to mind when they read each label. What do they know about Gamers? What do they think of Nerds or Slackers? Follow the activity with a discussion about stereotypes and assumptions that people have about groups of people. How do our assumptions influence our actions? How do these limit opportunities for ourselves and others?

COMPETENCY 10
UNDERSTAND THE CHANGING NATURE OF LIFE/WORK ROLES

LEVEL 3 (GRADES 9–12)

INDICATORS

Acquisition

10.3a1 Examine factors that have influenced the changing career patterns or paths of women and men

10.3a2 Examine gender stereotyping and bias in educational programs and work settings

10.3a3 Identify attitudes, behaviours and skills that contribute to eliminating gender bias and stereotyping

10.3a4 Investigate advantages and challenges of adopting non-traditional work roles

Application

10.3b1 Demonstrate attitudes, behaviours and skills that contribute to eliminating gender bias and stereotyping

Personalization

10.3c1 Determine one's desire to contribute to eliminating gender bias and stereotyping

10.3c2 Examine the possibility of adopting non-traditional work roles

10.3c3 Consider fulfilling work roles regardless of gender bias and stereotyping

Actualization

10.3d1 Create and engage in fulfilling life/work scenarios regardless of gender bias and stereotyping

SUGGESTIONS FOR INSTRUCTION

10.3a3 A Time When...

Have students work in groups to identify biases, stereotypes, and discriminatory behaviours that could limit opportunities for people.

Record examples of discriminatory situations on index cards and post them around the room. Have students read and think about each one. Have they ever been in such a situation, alone or with someone else? How did they feel? What did they do? Students can think about this quietly and respond individually. You could then invite students who are willing to share their responses. **Note:** Responses can be highly personal and sensitive and it may not be appropriate to have this as a public sharing activity.

Examples of discriminatory situations:

- A time when you were judged unfairly because of the friends you hung around with.
- A time when you were discriminated against because of your colour, height, size, or shape.
- A time when someone made an assumption about you based on how you looked.
- A time when a bias or stereotype limited your opportunity.
- A time where you were treated unequally or unfairly.
- A time when you were discriminated against because of your gender.

10.3b1 Rules to Live By.

Have students generate a list of non-discriminatory behaviours. What rules can they think of that would help to ensure that their attitudes and behaviours are non-discriminatory? Have students create posters to depict these "rules to live by."

COMPETENCY 11
UNDERSTAND, ENGAGE IN, AND MANAGE ONE'S OWN LIFE/WORK BUILDING PROCESS

LEVEL 1 (GRADES K–4)

INDICATORS

Acquisition

11.1a1 Explore the concept of *change is constant* and its relation to life and work

11.1a2 Explore the concept of *learning is an ongoing process* and its relation to life and work

11.1a3 Explore the concept of *following one's heart* and its relation to life and work

11.1a4 Explore the concept of *goal setting* as a source of inspiration and motivation in life and work

11.1a5 Understand the value of *focusing on the journey* in life and work

11.1a6 Discover the benefits of *strong relationships* to life and work

Application

11.1b1 Recognize situations of change and transformation in one's environment

11.1b2 Seek desired information and learn from different sources

11.1b3 Try new experiences according to one's dreams, personal values and interests

11.1b4 Plan and take part in an activity of interest and describe what one has learned during the activity

11.1b5 Identify one's set of relationships

Personalization

11.1c1 Examine one's opinions and feelings about change, learning, following one's heart, setting goals, focusing on the journey and having or developing a network of allies

Actualization

11.1d1 Engage in experiences that expose one to change, continuous learning, personal values and dreams, goal setting, journeys and networking

SUGGESTIONS FOR INSTRUCTION

11.1a2–11.1a4 Personal Milestones.

Have students create a timeline of personal milestones on chart paper or poster paper. What are all the things they have learned to do from birth to now? Limit students to about 6 milestones per year. Have them think about their learning accomplishments each year and add them to the timeline. Have students share their learning and discuss the concept of lifelong learning. On the bottom of the timeline, using different coloured pens or index cards, students can identify people who helped them achieve these learning milestones.

Provide students with cut-out hearts in red paper (see p. 216). Have students write their motivation for learning or achieving each milestone on a heart. For example, they might say that they learned to make model planes because they were fascinated with flying and travel. Have students attach their hearts to their timelines. Next, have students examine their own timelines individually or with a partner to look for connections, or bridges, to possible work roles. Provide students with cut-outs of bridges to add to their timelines (see p. 217). Students can write a work role on each bridge.

COMPETENCY 11

UNDERSTAND, ENGAGE IN, AND MANAGE ONE'S OWN LIFE/WORK BUILDING PROCESS

LEVEL 2 (GRADES 5–8)

INDICATORS

Acquisition

11.2a1 Explore the concept *every decision is a life/work decision*

11.2a2 Understand the concept of *life/work building*

11.2a3 Understand the difference between career planning and life/work building

11.2a4 Understand the importance of developing flexible and adaptable short-term action plans within the life/work building process

11.2a5 Understand the concept of a *preferred future* as part of the life/work building process

11.2a6 Understand the concept and importance of a *life/work portfolio*

Application

11.2b1 Define one's preferred future

11.2b2 Develop short-term action plans in step with one's preferred future

11.2b3 Create and maintain one's life/work portfolio

Personalization

11.2c1 Re-examine and assess one's preferred future using as criteria newly acquired information about self and the world of work

Actualization

11.2d1 Take steps to move toward one's preferred future

11.2d2 Adjust one's preferred future as experience changes one's knowledge of self

SUGGESTIONS FOR INSTRUCTION

11.2a2, 11.2a6   Life/Work Portfolio.

Discuss the concept of life/work building and the importance of collecting artifacts to keep track of important events. (You may want to have students complete Personal Milestones, p. 201, beforehand.) Building a portfolio of artifacts is a lifelong process. Certificates of achievement or completion, awards, work samples, and personal notes are all examples of what could be included in a portfolio. These items are all evidence of skills, knowledge, and behaviours that demonstrate life/work building.

Have students collect samples for a personal portfolio and compile these in either a digital or binder/book format. Goals and plans may change over time, but the samples students collect will be solid proof of skills and achievements throughout life.

COMPETENCY 11

UNDERSTAND, ENGAGE IN, AND MANAGE ONE'S OWN LIFE/WORK BUILDING PROCESS

LEVEL 3 (GRADES 9–12)

INDICATORS

Acquisition

11.3a1   Understand the concept of *work dynamic* and its relation to life/work building

11.3a2   Understand how risk-taking and positive attitudes towards self and work (flexibility, openness, positive uncertainty, etc.) are important to the life/work building process

11.3a3   Understand how information on self and on the work dynamic is important to the life/work building process

11.3a4   Explore the notion of *life/work scenario building* as an integral component of the life/work building process

11.3a5   Understand the importance of pursuing one's short-term action plans

Application

11.3b1   Demonstrate risk-taking and positive attitudes toward self and work (flexibility, openness, positive uncertainty, etc.)

11.3b2   Update one's portfolio using newly acquired information about self and the work dynamic

11.3b3   Build life/work scenarios in step with one's preferred future

11.3b4   Develop and pursue short-term action plans in light of one's desired life/work scenarios

11.3b5   Experience different roles through work experience, volunteering, social events, etc.

Personalization

11.3c1   Refine one's self-perception (based on life/work experiences) and evaluate its impact on one's decisions or choices

11.3c2   Revisit one's preferred future to determine whether or not it is necessary to modify and/or create new life/work scenarios and adjust one's short-term action plans

Actualization

11.3d1   Engage in a life/work building process that truly reflects self

SUGGESTIONS FOR INSTRUCTION

11.3a2 Attitudes and Actions.

Discuss positive and negative attitudes towards self and work. What kinds of attitudes and actions build bridges (positive) and what kinds of attitudes and actions burn bridges (negative)? Examples:

Build Bridges	Burn Bridges
being flexible	talking behind people's backs
being optimistic	posting inappropriate comments online
being honest	being dishonest
helping others	not engaging with others

11.3c1, 11.3c2   Retirement Speech.

Have students think about the kind of person they want to be and the way they want to be remembered. Consider information they have gathered about themselves and what they want for their future. How do they want to be remembered? What do they want people to say about them? What do they want to be known for? What do they hope to achieve? Ask students to write their own retirement speech. Ask them to think about whether it is noble, whether it will help them strive for success, and how much it will inspire them. Have them write the speech and keep it in the back of their life/work portfolio (see Life/Work Portfolio, p. 203) where they can revisit it periodically to contemplate whether they are still working towards who they want to be. While this can be a very individual activity, some students may elect to share their speech with the class.

QUILT

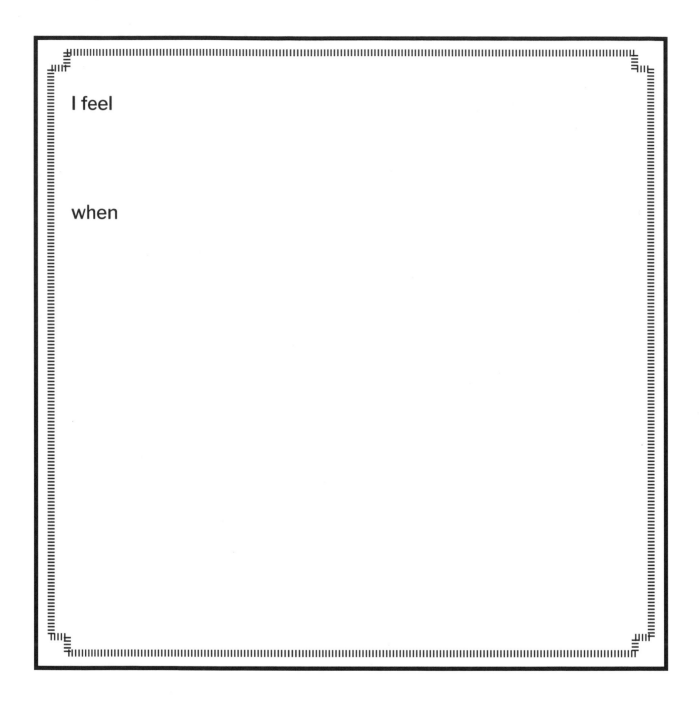

I feel

when

SQUARE PUZZLE

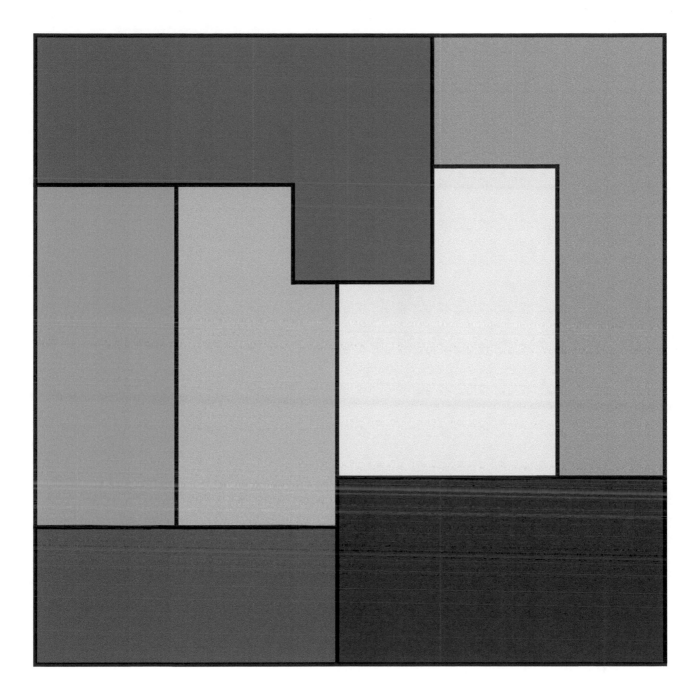

SQUARE PUZZLE – BLANK TEMPLATE

MY HEALTH JOURNAL

This week		
I made healthy choices	I shared feelings	I asked for help with...
Reflections	Reflections	Reflections

This week

Wishes, ideas, goals

PERSONAL AND PROFESSIONAL GOALS

Personal Goal:

_____

Professional Goal:

_____

What I'm doing to achieve my goal

What I'm doing that's getting in the way of my goal

What else can help me achieve my goal?

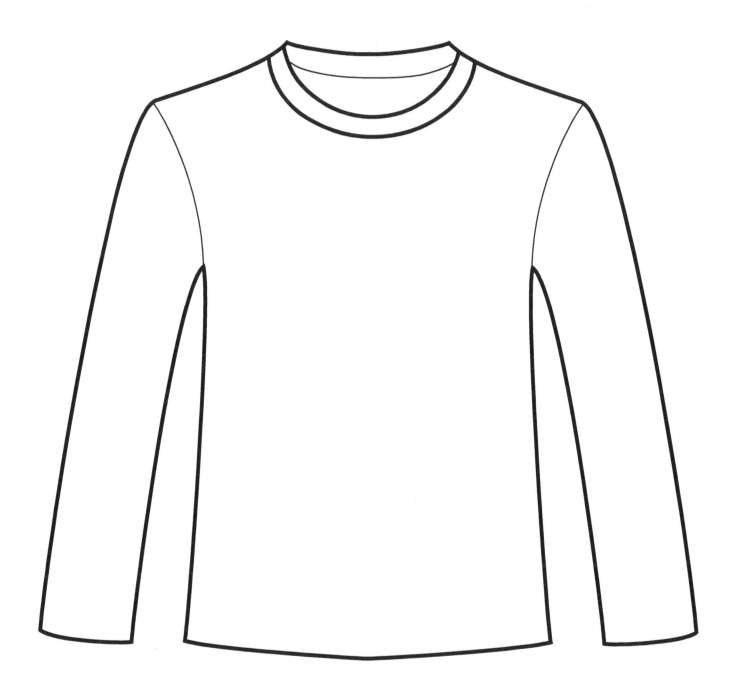

TOWER OF SUCCESS

My full potential

Me as a member of society

Me in the community

Me at school

Me at home

Me

DETECTIVE GLASS

What happened?

Who is involved?

When did it happen?

Where did it happen?

How did it happen?

Why did it happen?

INSIDE AND OUTSIDE THE HOME

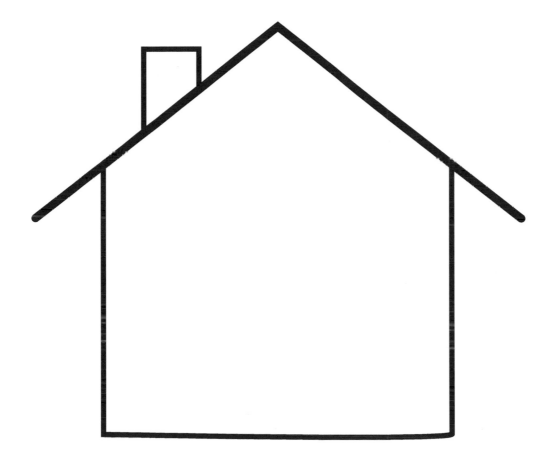

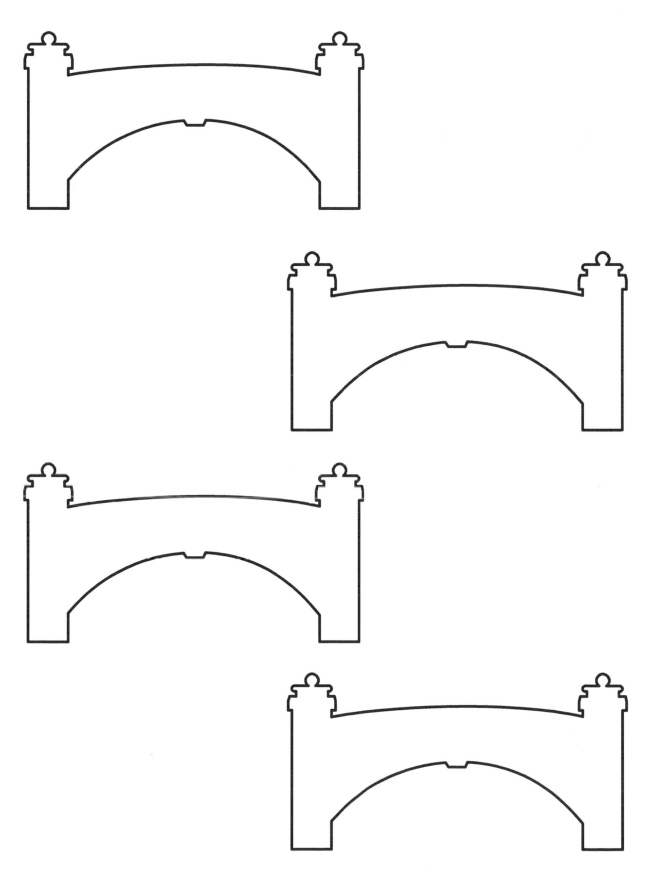

APPENDIX

● ● ● ● ●

OPTIMIZING WELL-BEING AND RESPONDING TO EMOTIONAL DISTRESS OF CHILDREN AND YOUTH

GENERAL GUIDELINES AND CONSIDERATIONS FOR SERVICE PROVIDERS:

Refugee families will be affected by their trauma related experiences, and by losses and adaptations related to settlement. Overall, these children and families are resilient. However, it is expected that children might exhibit a range of behavioural signs of distress ranging from mild to, in a few circumstances, severe.

The following information should be considered to support children and youth who are refugees:

- A period of at least 3 to 6 months for 'adaptation' and stabilization to new circumstances is expected.

- Parents generally will know if their child's behaviour is unusual or concerning.

- First and foremost, children who are experiencing distress should be cared for by parents and natural community supports.

- Involvement of formal mental health services should occur when levels of distress are extreme, prolonged, significantly interfering, and/or resulting in a concern of harm to self or others. Services should occur in a consultative, collaborative, culturally informed, and where possible, family-focused manner.

- Safety and a sense of security and trust are the most important goals for children and their families.

- Provide consistent, predictable pattern of activities for the day. Explain planned activities that are to come in a calm and organized fashion.

- Be nurturing and comforting – take cues from the child about physical displays of affection.

- Listen to what children and their parents tell you they need. If children want to talk about their past experiences, don't be afraid to listen, provide comfort and support, and answer questions as best as you can.

- Let children know what you expect from them and what they can expect from you.

- Talk and provide information in an age-appropriate way. Unpredictability and the "unknown" are likely to increase anxiety and fearfulness.

- Provide age appropriate choice and control.

- Certain ethnocultural groups may use indirect expressions of distress when asked about well-being. Often body related metaphors are used. In language translation, these may be communicated as follows:

    - A range of emotional symptoms or relationship problems may be expressed as being "tired" or having a "tired psyche."
    - Fear and anxiety may be expressed as "falling or crumbling of the heart," or "my heart is squeezing".
    - Helplessness, hopelessness or depression may be described as "the world is closing in front of my face", "the world became dark in front of me."

- Suicidality may be a source of stigma, shame and social exclusion. Disclosure regarding suicidal thoughts is more likely to be indirect, for example, wishing for sleep and not to wake up.

CHILDREN AND YOUTH: SIGNS OF DISTRESS AND WAYS TO RESPOND

When the following symptoms and behaviours are ongoing and severe enough that they cause significant impact on the child's or youth's functioning, mental health, and/or addictions services, should be sought.

Birth to Five Years of Age	
Some common things you may see or hear	Some ways of responding
· Clinging to parent/care provider	· Provide comfort and predictability
· Unusual crying or tantrums	· Avoid long separations
· Thumb sucking or nail-biting	· Put names to feelings
· Bedwetting not previously present	· Be patient and understanding
· Fear of dark or sleeping alone	· Redirect from inappropriate behaviours to acceptable ones in a calm accepting way
· Hitting or biting	
· Unable to sit still	· Create calming bedtime routines and plans for sleep disruption
· Passiveness, withdrawn or silent for long periods	· Reassurance of safety
· Play containing war/danger themes and symbols	· Help name feelings and communicate acceptance of difficult feelings

Six to Twelve Years of Age

Some common things you may see or hear	Some ways of responding
• Sleep disturbance – nightmares and/or fear of dark	• Create calming activities before bed
• Repeated storytelling and play related to trauma	• Limit exposure to television and games that may trigger fear and anxiety
• Angry and aggressive outbursts	• Let child talk about bad dreams and, when appropriate, redirect to more pleasant and calming thoughts so s/he can more easily fall asleep
• Loss of interest in activities	• Allow child to talk about and act out reactions to trauma
• School refusal	
• Difficulties with concentration and social relations	• Normalize reactions
• Regression to behaviours common in younger ages	• Create opportunities to talk about school and relationships
• Physical symptoms such as vomiting, stomach aches and/or headaches	• Ensure no medical basis to physical symptoms
	• Provide healthy food options
	• Ensure adequate eating and sleeping

Thirteen to Seventeen Years of Age

Some common things you may see or hear	Some ways of responding
• Conflict at home and/or at school	• Spend time talking about stresses on relationships and stresses of the transitions and changes
• Sleep and eating problems	
• Deterioration in school performance	• Normalize and validate feelings
• Rapidly changing relationships	• Discuss dangers of high risk behaviours
• Heightened sibling aggression or protectiveness	• Increase contact and knowledge of youth's activities
• Extreme risk taking	
• Significant substance abuse	• Provide opportunity for family activity and positive community activity
• Social withdrawal or withdrawal from family	• Monitor suicidal thoughts (ex: frequency, intensity, intent, plan, means)
• Suicidal/homicidal thoughts	
	• Referral to appropriate addiction agency or treatment

CHILDREN AND YOUTH: EMERGENCY IMMEDIATE INTERVENTION IS REQUIRED

These signs may mean there is imminent risk of harm to self or others.

Some common things you may see or hear	Action
· Threatening to hurt or kill him or herself, or talking of wanting to hurt or kill him/herself	**· USE EMERGENCY RESOURCES:**
· Looking for ways to kill him/herself by seeking access to firearms, available pills, or other means	· Call 911 for immediate mental health and/or addictions help or transport to nearest hospital emergency department for medical intervention
· Talking or writing about death, dying or suicide, when these actions are out of the ordinary	· Contact local youth mental health mobile crisis team (if available) http://www.gov.mb.ca/healthyliving/mh/crisis.html
· Disorientation (not knowing their name, where they are from, not making sense)	· Call the Manitoba Suicide Line 1-877-435-7170

The following are additional Refugee Mental Health and Addictions Fact Sheets for Service Providers that complement this resource:

- Refugee Mental Health and Addictions Fact Sheet for Service Providers: Optimizing Well-being and Responding to Emotional Distress of Adults

- Refugee Mental Health and Addictions Fact Sheet for Service Providers: Mental Health and Addictions Services for Refugees

GUIDING PRINCIPLES FOR SUPPORTING NEWCOMER AND REFUGEE STUDENTS

The following is an excerpt from "A Culture of Care and Compassion for Refugee Students: Creating a State of *nhân đạo*" by Jan Stewart, *Education Canada*, Vol. 57 (1), March 2017, Canadian Education Association, https://www.edcan.ca/articles/a-culture-of-care-and-compassion-for-refugee-students/.

KNOW YOUR STUDENTS

Take the time to learn about where your students come from and acknowledge their past. Be open to hearing their personal story, but remember that behind the trauma story is the story of courage and survival. See students with an "asset perspective" instead of a "deficit perspective." Help reorient students to focus on the skills, resources and power that they have to get through difficult times. View each student who comes to school as having unique experiences and backgrounds that are worthy of celebrating.

KNOW AND BUILD YOUR COMMUNITY

Approach teaching and learning from a sociocultural and humanistic perspective and aim to create the kind of learning spaces and opportunities to connect the head and the heart. Teachers, school staff, students, and the community need to collaborate with each other, have a willingness to hear different perspectives, and a readiness to take risks to try new approaches. Invite community members in to organize after school clubs or a lunch hour activity. Have a designated "community room" where staff, students, and the community can come together to discuss current issues and plan future events.

KNOW THE SIGNS

Students who are coping with distressing events and experiences might display hyperarousal, avoidance, withdrawal, or disassociation. They might be easily over-stimulated and lack a readiness to learn. Communicating and self-expression may be difficult and problem-solving and decision-making may be compromised. Students who have experienced trauma may have difficulty regulating emotions; you might see a state of calmness one moment and anxiety or anger the next moment. Fear and concern for their own safety or the safety of their family members may occupy their thoughts. If a student is feeling threatened in your classroom, there will be little learning. You simply cannot ignore trauma or teach it away. A sense of security and trust are the foundation for providing support to students; once safety has been established, the process of healing can begin. Healing takes time and the process of settling and adjustment can take years. Listen to what students and parents tell you they need, and know that some will talk and others will not. Be open to listening and providing comfort and support.

KNOW WHO CAN HELP

Know when to refer to the next level of care. If you have concerns about the safety of the student or the safety of others, refer to the next level of care. If you have a "gut feeling" that something is wrong, trust your instincts and get additional support. A counsellor or therapist may need to be involved when you see serious changes in behaviour, or when the student talks or writes about death, dying or suicide. Significant substance abuse and heightened aggression or protectiveness are also signs that the student needs more support. Work with the student's family or caregivers and ensure that you are working together to support the student.

When there are cultural issues that you may need to consult others about, seek out the help of a cultural broker or support worker. Settlement agencies and community groups can be a tremendous support to school staff and when the various systems are connected and working together, a more holistic and supportive environment is created. Link to mental health professionals in your community and know who you can go to for help or guidance. Welcome assistance into your school and classroom—there are many support people in the community who are ready and willing to help out.

KNOW YOURSELF

Working with refugee students can be rewarding and also extremely difficult. Invariably there will be a personal impact on an individual from hearing about the trauma, torture, violence and persecution inflicted on others. It is common to feel helpless and overwhelmed. It can be extremely distressing to hear about the violations to children and to hear the impact this had had on a child's life. Complicating this are the realities of the ongoing challenges after moving to a host country. For some, the trajectory is not always positive and for many teachers, it can seem like an overwhelming task to support the increasing numbers of students who are dealing with various forms of trauma. In some cases, you may be the only support in a student's life and this can be a tremendous feeling of responsibility. Know your personal signs of stress and distress and know when, and how, to look after your own mental health.

Supporting children from refugee backgrounds can be a challenging journey and it can also be a process of renewed hope and opportunity. Creating a safe space that is sensitive to the unique, and sometimes disruptive, past of children requires care and commitment. A new start offers refugee students hope and promise for a better future. If we do the work, schools can provide an environment of care and compassion that fosters acceptance and supports the successful integration of Canada's newest citizens.

KNOWLEDGE CHAMPIONS

A SPECIAL THANK YOU TO OUR KNOWLEDGE CHAMPIONS FOR CAREER DEVELOPMENT WHO HELPED TO MAKE POSSIBLE THE PUBLICATION OF THIS GUIDE.

CERIC

CERIC is a charitable organization that advances education and research in career counselling and career development, in order to increase the economic and social well-being of Canadians. It funds projects to develop innovative resources that build the knowledge and skills of diverse career professionals. CERIC also annually hosts Cannexus, Canada's largest bilingual career development conference, publishes the country's only peer-reviewed journal, *Canadian Journal of Career Development*, and runs the free ContactPoint / OrientAction online communities, which provide learning and networking in the career field. **ceric.ca**

INTERNATIONAL CENTRE FOR INNOVATION IN EDUCATION (ICIE)

The International Centre for Innovation in Education (ICIE) has roles to play in expanding and strengthening gifted education and excellence throughout the world. It provides vibrant global, cross-cultural forums for sharing, networking, and empowering every person to become a responsible, self-directed, lifelong learner through a positive partnership of families, teachers, scholars, universities, NGOs, ministries of education and community. The ICIE is committed to the development of all students and teachers as productive world citizens and leaders for the future. We challenge you to join us in this endeavour. **icieworld.net**

UNIVERSITY OF WINNIPEG'S FACULTY OF EDUCATION

The University of Winnipeg's Faculty of Education offers a unique integrated education program that allows students to work towards a Bachelor of Arts, Science, or Kinesiology while completing a Bachelor of Education Degree. The Faculty also offers a Post Baccalaureate Diploma in Education for in-service teacher development and continuing education in school counselling, inclusive education and general studies. **uwinnipeg.ca/education**

REFERENCES

American Psychiatric Association. (2013). *Diagnostic and statistical manual of mental disorders,* 5th Ed. Washington, DC: Author.

American Psychological Association. (2008). *Children and Trauma: Update for mental health professionals.* Retrieved from http://www.apa.org/pi/families/resources/children-trauma-update. aspx

Brar, N. (2010). *Bridging the gap: Educational cultural brokers supporting the mental health of refugee youth.* Calgary, AB: University of Alberta Press.

Brar-Josan, N., & Yohani, S. C. (2014). A framework for counsellor–cultural broker collaboration. *Canadian Journal of Counselling and Psychotherapy, 48*(2). Retrieved from http://cjc-rcc.ucalgary.ca/cjc/ index.php/rcc/article/view/2660

Bronfenbrenner, U. (2001). The bioecological theory of human development. In N. J. Smelser & P. B. Baltes (Eds.), *International encyclopedia of the social and behavioural sciences* (Vol. 10, pp. 6963–6970). New York: Elsevier.

Canadian Council for Career Development. (2012). *The Canadian standards and guidelines for career development practitioners.* Retrieved from http://cccda.org/cccda/index.php/certification/canadi-an-standards-guidelines-for-career-development-practitioners-sg

Canadian Paediatric Society. (2016). *Post-traumatic stress disorder* [Web page]. Retrieved from Caring for Kids New To Canada website: http://www.kidsnewtocanada.ca/mental-health/ptsd

Cole, S. F., O'Brien J. G., Gadd, M. G., Ristuccia, J., Wallace D. L., & Gregory, M. (2005). *Helping traumatized children learn: Supportive school environments for children traumatized by family violence.* Massachusetts Advocates for Children. Retrieved from https://traumasensitiveschools.org/ wp-content/uploads/2013/06/Helping-Traumatized-Children-Learn.pdf

Diehl, L. M. (2013, October 15). Children and trauma: How schools can help with healing. *The Brown University Child and Adolescent Behavior Letter.* Retrieved from http://www.childadolescentbe-havior.com/Article-Detail/children-and-trauma-how-schools-can-help-with-healing.aspx

Ehntholt, K. A., & Yule, W. (2006) Practitioner review: Assessment and treatment of refugee children and adolescents who have experienced war-related trauma. *Journal of Child Psychology and Psychiatry, 47*(12), 1197–1210.

Elez, T. (2014). Restoring hope: Responding to career concerns of immigrant clients. *The Canadian Journal of Career Development, 13*(1), 32–45.

Fallot, R., & Harris, M. (Eds.) (2001). *Using trauma theory to design service systems.* New Directions for Mental Health Services. San Francisco: Jossey-Bass.

Fazel, M., Wheeler, J., & Danesh, J. (2005). Prevalence of serious mental disorder in 7000 refugees resettled in western countries: A systematic review. *Lancet, 365*(9467), 1309–1314.

Gardner, H. (2004). *Frames of mind: the theory of multiple intelligences.* New York: Basic Books.

Haché, L., Redekopp, D. E., & Jarvis, P. S. (2006). *Blueprint for life/work designs: The quick reference guide.* National LifeWork Centre. Retrieved from http://www.nlsd113.com/ckfinder/userfiles/files/ Career_Education/Blueprint_for_Life_-_Quick_REFERENCE_GUIDE.pdf

Health Canada. (2002). *The report on mental illness in Canada.* Retrieved from http://www.phac-aspc. gc.ca/publicat/miic-mmac/pdf/men_ill_e.pdf

Hodes, M. (2000). Psychologically distressed refugee children in the United Kingdom. *Child Psychology and Psychiatry Review, 5*(2), 57–68.

Kilpatrick, D. G., Ruggiero, K. J., Acierno, R., Saunders, B. E. Resnick, H. S., & Best, C. L. (2003). Violence and risk of PTSD, major depression, substance abuse/dependence, and comorbidity: Results from the National Survey of Adolescents. *Journal of Consulting and Clinical Psychology, 71*(4), 692–700.

Kirmayer, L. J., Narasiah, L. J., Munoz, M., Rashid, M., Ryder, A. G., Guzder, J., Hassan, G., Rousseau, C., & Pottie, K. (2011). Common mental health problems in immigrants and refugees: General approach in primary care. *Canadian Medical Association Journal. 183*(12). http://www.cmaj.ca/content/183/12/ E959.full

MacNevin, J. (2012). Learning the way: Teaching and learning with and for youth from refugee backgrounds in Prince Edward Island. *Canadian Journal of Education, 35*(3), 48–63.

McCluskey, K. & McCluskey, A. (2001). *ADHD: Our personal journey.* Winnipeg, MB: Portage and Main Press.

Mollica, R. F. (2011). Introduction. In R. F. Mollica (Ed.), *Global mental health: trauma and recovery: A companion guide for field and clinical care of traumatized people worldwide* (pp. 13–43). Cambridge, MA: Harvard Program in Refugee Trauma.

Mollica, R. F. (2016, November). 11-Point Tool-Kit: Healing the wounds of mass violence. Content presented by Richard Mollica as part of a lecture in the Global Mental Health: Trauma and Recovery Program through Harvard Medical School. Porano, Italy.

Mollica, R. F., Brooks, R. T., Ekblad, S., & McDonald, L. (2015). The new H5 model of refugee trauma and recovery. In J. Lindert & I. Levav (Eds.), V*iolence and mental health.* Springer, Dordrecht. Retrieved from http://link.springer.com/chapter/10.1007/978-94-017- 8999-8_16

National Center for Cultural Competence (NCCC). (2004). *Bridging the cultural divide in health care settings: The essential role of cultural broker programs.* National Center for Cultural Competence, Georgetown University Center for Child and Human Development. Retrieved from https://nccc. georgetown.edu/documents/Cultural_Broker_Guide_English.pdf

National Child Traumatic Stress Network. (2008, October). *Child trauma toolkit for educators.* Los Angeles, CA & Durham, NC: National Center for Child Traumatic Stress. Retrieved from https:// wmich.edu/sites/default/files/attachments/u57/2013/child-trauma-toolkit.pdf

National Child Traumatic Stress Network. (2017). *The effects of trauma on schools and learning* [Web page]. Retrieved from the National Child Traumatic Stress Network website: http://www.nctsn.org/resources/audiences/school-personnel/effects-of-trauma

National LifeWork Centre. (2010). *Blueprint for lifework designs.* Memramcook, NB. Retrieved from http://www.lifework.ca/lifework/index.html

Newfoundland and Labrador Department of Education and Early Childhood Development. (n.d.). *A School-wide approach: positive behaviour supports.* Retrieved from http://www.ed.gov.nl.ca/edu/k12/safeandcaring/teachers/pbs/PositiveBehaviourSupports.pdf

Ovando, C., Collier, V., & Combs, M. (2003). *Bilingual and ESL classrooms: Teaching multicultural contexts.* New York: McGraw-Hill.

Public Health Agency of Canada. (2010). *Canadian Incidence Study of Reported Child Abuse and Neglect – 2008: Major Findings.* Retrieved from http://cwrp.ca/sites/default/files/publications/en/CIS-2008-rprt-eng.pdf

Ricento, T. (2013). Measuring success when English isn't your native language. In P. Siemund, I. Gogolin, M. Schulz, & J. Davydova (Eds.), *Multilingualism and language diversity in urban areas* (pp. 349–368). Amsterdam: John Benjamins Publishing Co.; Philadelphia, PA: John Benjamins North America.

Russell, S. S. (2002, November 1). Refugees: Risks and challenges worldwide. *Migration Information Source.* Retrieved from http://www.migrationpolicy.org/article/refugees-risks-and-challenges-worldwide

Scheeringa, M. (2013). *PTSD for children 6 years and younger* [Web page]. National Center for PTSD, U.S. Department of Veterans Affairs. Retrieved from http://www.ptsd.va.gov/professional/PTSD-overview/ptsd_children_6_and_younger.asp

Stewart, J. (2011). *Supporting refugee children: Strategies for educators.* Toronto, ON: University of Toronto Press.

Stewart, J. (2014). The school counsellor's role in promoting social justice for children from refugee and immigrant backgrounds. *Canadian Journal of Counselling and Psychotherapy, 48*(3), 251–269.

Stewart, J. (2016, Spring). Supporting refugee children: Tips for teachers who want to CARE. *Manitoba School Counsellor,* 10–11.

Stewart, J. (2017a). A culture of care and compassion for refugee students: Creating a sense of *nhân đạo. Education Canada, 57* (1). Retrieved from http://www.cea-ace.ca/education-canada/article/culture-care-and-compassion-refugee-students

Stewart, J. (2017b, June 27). War, terror, neglect: How Canadian schools could tackle child trauma. *The Conversation.* Retrieved from https://theconversation.com/war-terror-neglect-how-canadian-schools-could-tackle-child-trauma-78448

Sunderland, A., & Findlay, L. C. (2013). *Perceived need for mental health care in Canada: Results from the 2012 Canadian community health survey – Mental health.* Statistics Canada. Retrieved from https://www.mooddisorders.ca/sites/mooddisorders.ca/files/downloads/mentalhealth_statcan11863-eng.pdf

Thomas, W., & Collier, V. (1997). *School effectiveness for language minority students.* Washington, DC: National Clearinghouse for Bilingual Education, George Washington University, Center for the Study of Language and Education.

United Nations High Commissioner for Refugees (UNHCR). (2017). *Global trends: Forced displacement in 2016.* Geneva: UNHCR. Retrieved from http://www.unhcr.org/globaltrends2016/

Yohani, S. C. (2010). *Challenges and opportunities for educational cultural brokers in facilitating the school adaptation of refugee children.* Prairie Metropolis Centre: Working Paper Series. Retrieved from https://sites.ualberta.ca/~pcerii/WorkingPapers/Working%20papers%20from%20June,%202009/WP10-05.pdf

PRAISE FOR *BRIDGING TWO WORLDS: SUPPORTING NEWCOMER AND REFUGEE YOUTH*

"*Bridging Two Worlds* brings to bear the power of original research and the insight of its experienced authors on the crucial issue of educating newcomers. With the world witnessing an ever-growing number of refugees – many coming to our shores with expectations of a better life – education is the key. Equally, the new arrivals must learn about their new land and how they can make Canada a better place. Fortunately, this guide creates understanding and provides the tools that will enable the building of bridges to take place."
- *Hon. Lloyd Axworthy, Chair, World Council on Refugees and Former Canadian Minister of Foreign Affairs*

"Grounded in solid research and underpinned by values of diversity and inclusivity, this timely publication is brimming with practical lesson plans and instructional resources. This is an absolute must-read for educators and others seeking to welcome and support newcomers and refugee families."
- *Sareena Hopkins, Executive Director, Canadian Career Development Foundation*

"New Brunswick educators have benefitted from Dr. Stewart's work and we believe that her unique experiences, vast insight and depth of knowledge in this area is unparalleled in our country. The comprehensive information and data-informed materials, including lesson plans to build teacher capacity and case studies for analysis, will be essential resources for educational leaders across the country as they plan for their increasingly diverse classrooms and schools."
- *Kathy Whynot, English as Additional Language & Newcomer Children and Youth Learning Specialist, Department of Education & Early Childhood Development, Government of New Brunswick*

"A well-researched and much-needed resource for educators and school counsellors who support newcomers and refugee youth. A must-have book for the toolkit of those working with newcomer and refugee youth or for those who need to understand this emerging career decision-making area."
- *John Driscoll, President, Canadian Counselling and Psychotherapy Association*

"Jan Stewart and Lorna Martin have written a comprehensive guide for cultural sensitivity in Canadian school systems. *Bridging Two Worlds: Supporting Newcomer and Refugee Youth* provides practical information that builds the capacity of teachers to support newcomers and refugees in the classroom. Organizations such as ours can use this guide as a resource to develop the core competencies needed for inclusive settlement work. I truly believe this well-written and informative book should be essential reading for government, teachers and settlement practitioners across Alberta and the country."
- *Milton Ortega, Executive Director, Alberta Association of Immigrant Serving Agencies*

"*Bridging Two Worlds* excels in clearly connecting research with practical, culturally responsive career development activities. It is a tremendous resource for deepening my own understanding as an educator and supporting learners with their career development."
- *Celia Vielfaure, Career & Workforce Development Services Advisor, Manitoba Institute for Trades and Technology*

"*Bridging Two Worlds* is a well-written, articulate and comprehensive guide for all education professionals who work with newcomer and refugee children and youth. From creating a welcoming classroom to incorporating strategies like storytelling to career development planning, this resource covers all the bases in providing professionals a relevant and useful tool to help ensure the successful integration of this population of students. This book will become a staple resource for my team as we support our schools in their work with newcomer and refugee learners."
- *Christine Oliver, Supervisor, English Language Learning, Kingsland Reception Centre, Calgary Board of Education*

"With the growing number of newcomer and refugee children and youth settling in Canada who have experienced trauma, this book represents an excellent resource to those current and future educators, settlement workers and healthcare practitioners who are working, or will be working, with such a vulnerable population. I recommend it highly. "
- *James Baker, PhD, Banting Postdoctoral Fellow, Department of Sociology, McMaster University and Manager, Programs and Research, Association for New Canadians, Newfoundland and Labrador*

"*Bridging Two Worlds: Supporting Newcomer and Refugee Youth* is an invaluable guide to curriculum implementation and integration based on a rigorous, three-year research program. Importantly, the guide includes 30 detailed lesson plans designed to foster core competencies to help teachers effectively address the needs of newcomer and refugee children and youth. These include a powerful "privilege walk" designed to heighten awareness of the social and economic inequality faced by newcomers. If you are interested in building culturally responsive bridges in the school system, this book will be an invaluable resource."
- *Leah Hamilton, PhD, Associate Professor; Bissett School of Business, Research Development Officer; Office of Research, Scholarship and Community Engagement, Mount Royal University*